Governance for health equity

taking forward the equity values and goals of Health 2020 in the WHO European Region

Chris Brown
Dominic Harrison
Harry Burns
Erio Ziglio

ABSTRACT

This report is one of 13 task group reports which underpin the work of the European review of the social determinants of health and the health divide. The study was commissioned by the WHO Regional Office for Europe to inform the development of Health 2020. With its distilled lessons, this publication is of vital importance for the WHO European Region's 53 Member States and their efforts to implement the equity goals of Health 2020. It provides a situation analysis of why policies and interventions to address social determinants of health and health inequities succeed or fail. It also discusses important features of governance and delivery systems that increase likely success in reducing inequities. A systems checklist for governing for health equity as a whole-of-government approach is put forward. This is intended for further discussion and as a framework to support strengthening how countries govern for health equity in practice, through action on social determinants.

Keywords

Health Management and Planning, Health policy, Health services accessibility, Health status disparities, Public health, Socioeconomic factors

---

Address requests about publications of the WHO Regional Office for Europe to:

    Publications
    WHO Regional Office for Europe
    UN City, Marmorvej 51
    DK-2100 Copenhagen Ø, Denmark

Alternatively, complete an online request form for documentation, health information, or for permission to quote or translate, on the Regional Office web site (http://www.euro.who.int/pubrequest).

ISBN 9789289000550
© World Health Organization 2013, updated reprint 2014

All rights reserved. The Regional Office for Europe of the World Health Organization welcomes requests for permission to reproduce or translate its publications, in part or in full.

The designations employed and the presentation of the material in this publication do not imply the expression of any opinion whatsoever on the part of the World Health Organization concerning the legal status of any country, territory, city or area or of its authorities, or concerning the delimitation of its frontiers or boundaries. Dotted lines on maps represent approximate border lines for which there may not yet be full agreement.

The mention of specific companies or of certain manufacturers' products does not imply that they are endorsed or recommended by the World Health Organization in preference to others of a similar nature that are not mentioned. Errors and omissions excepted, the names of proprietary products are distinguished by initial capital letters.

All reasonable precautions have been taken by the World Health Organization to verify the information contained in this publication. However, the published material is being distributed without warranty of any kind, either express or implied. The responsibility for the interpretation and use of the material lies with the reader. In no event shall the World Health Organization be liable for damages arising from its use. The views expressed by authors, editors, or expert groups do not necessarily represent the decisions or the stated policy of the World Health Organization.

CONTENTS

Acknowledgements	vi
Foreword	vii
Authors	x
Abbreviations	xi
Executive summary	1
1. Health inequities in the WHO European Region	**3**
1.1. Health inequities in Europe	3
2. Trends in governance thinking and practice	**8**
2.1. Reducing inequities in health through action on social determinants – why governance is important	8
2.2. Reasons for acting on social determinants and reducing health inequities	13
2.2.1. Reducing preventable ill health is a matter of fairness and social justice	13
2.2.2. Health is a human right	13
2.2.3. Health is a public good	16
2.2.4. Loss of health and increasing health inequity lead to social conflict and undermines community cohesion	16
2.2.5. Population health is an economic asset and a productive good	17
2.3. Summary of key issues in governance for health equity	18
2.4. Summary of the main principles of effective governance for health equity	20
3. Progress and responses in Europe	**25**
3.1. Integrated policies capable of acting on social determinants	25
3.2. Instruments that incentivize collaboration across stakeholders and hold decision-makers to account	26
3.2.1. Horizontal and vertical integration of actions	28

3.3. Active participation and engagement of communities ... 29

4. Why governance and delivery fail ... 31

4.1. Conceptual failure ... 31

4.2. Delivery chain failure ... 36
4.2.1. Reliance on small-scale project and pilots ... 36
4.2.2. Lack of appropriate incentives and mechanisms for acting across sectors and determinants ... 37
4.2.3. Lack of investment in ongoing assessment of trends in inequities and social determinants ... 39
4.2.4. Gaps in quality and type of data/intelligence ... 39

4.3. Governmental control strategy failure ... 41

4.4. Public health system failure ... 43

5. Systems checklist for governing for health equity through action on social determinants of health ... 46

5.1. Characteristics of delivery systems important to reducing inequities through action on social determinants of health ... 50

6. Recommendations ... 52

6.1. Promote and ensure shared responsibility for equity results across government ... 52
6.1.1. Strengthening the mix and coherence of instruments which enable and reward joint action on social inequities (i) across sectoral portfolios and (ii) between local, regional and national governments ... 52

6.2. Accountability instruments and capacities for equity ... 53

6.3. Equity and health equity as indicators of a fair and sustainable society ... 55

6.4. Involving local people and communities improves the design 56
and impact of policies and investments aimed at improving health
and reducing social inequities

6.5. Europe-wide information exchange 57

7. References 58

8. Bibliography 62

ACKNOWLEDGEMENTS

The authors would like to acknowledge the valuable inputs drawn from the work of co-authors of the WHO Regional Office for Europe *Resource guide on governance for social determinants of health and health inequities*: specifically, Jane Jenson (University of Montreal), Rene Loewenson (Training and Research Support Centre, Zimbabwe), Linda Marks (Durham University) and Helen Roberts (University College London Institute of Child Health).

Thanks are due for the valuable feedback received from external reviewers, including Professor Margaret Whitehead (WHO Collaborating Centre for Policy Research on Social Determinants of Health, University of Liverpool), Dr Johanna Hanefeld (London School of Hygiene and Tropical Medicine) and the governance team of the WHO Regional Office for Europe: specifically, Dr Hans Kluge and Dr Juan Eduardo Tello.

The authors would also like to acknowledge the contribution of WHO Regional Office for Europe heads of country offices in Kyrgyzstan, Mr Oskonbek Moldokulov; Poland, Dr Paulina Marianna Miskiewicz; Slovakia, Dr Darina Sedlakova; and Slovenia, Dr Marijan Ivanusa for their support in terms of case study validation and extend thanks to Tone Poulsson Torgersen (Norwegian Directorate of Health, Oslo) and David Pattison (Health Scotland, Edinburgh) for reviewing the illustrative examples relating to Norway and Scotland.

The WHO European Office for Investment for Health and Development wishes to thank the Department of Health England (United Kingdom) for the financial support provided for this publication.

A special acknowledgement is made to Gordon Sugden for his support and inspiration during the writing of the report.

FOREWORD

Addressing the social determinants of health and tackling health inequities in the WHO European Region is central to Health 2020 – the new European policy for health.

This publication is one of 13 task group reports which underpin the work of the *European review of the social determinants of health and the health divide*. The study was commissioned by the WHO Regional Office for Europe to inform the development of Health 2020. With its distilled lessons, this publication is of vital importance for the WHO European Region's 53 Member States and their efforts to implement the equity goals of Health 2020.

The findings of this report add to the recent increased understanding that health equity is a shared responsibility, requiring the engagement of all sectors of government and all segments of society. We have learnt from the *European review of the social determinants of health and the health divide* that a clear gradient exists in the health of the European population, in virtually every Member State. These inequalities can accumulate over the life course and are often perpetuated across generations, leading to persistent shortfalls in health and development potential in families, in communities and in our societies.

We have been reminded that these inequities and their social and economic costs pose a direct challenge to the attainment of values such as solidarity and social cohesion, which are core principles underpinning Health 2020.

Inside this publication, readers will find examples of practical experiences, promising practices and lessons learned on how to ensure that the promotion of health and the reduction of health inequities can be operationalized as a whole-of-government approach. Many useful cases and much evidence are presented to clearly demonstrate how coherent actions across social determinants can produce benefits for many policy sectors, not only for health, and how this further reinforces the value of health equity as a public good.

However, sustainable action to promote population health cannot be achieved only through individual action, or disjointed health topic programmes. The biggest challenge to achieving equitable gains in population health and securing health as a resource for overall development now rests with addressing the governance and/or system weaknesses described in this report: specifically, those which stem from observed common failures in the capacity of European policies to reduce inequities and in the governance systems which underpin policy implementation and accountability. Analysis of these issues reveals once again the kind of political commitment, professional expertise and engagement of civil society that must be fostered and sustained in order to improve performance and reduce inequities in health.

Making this happen requires an optimal mix of instruments to incentivize cooperation between many partners and sectors and to enable a coordinated approach to resourcing the research into – as well as the implementation and review of – the social determinants of health and equity goals.

Through Health 2020, this is being addressed by advocating strong **governance for health** as one of the pillars for the implementation of the new framework, and I am pleased to see that this report is also based on that notion. The report is valuable in identifying and advocating new know-how and instruments to strengthen our systems in governing better for health equity.

We already have good analytical epidemiological methods to **measure the problem** of health inequities caused by social factors. We already have good tools to **describe the problem** of health inequities and their social causation. We urgently need appropriate know-how to develop and implement **solutions** to this problem.

I refer specifically to the know-how needed to:

- effectively and efficiently integrate health equity goals into broader country development objectives;

- reinforce such integration through structural mechanisms, such as financing and investment frameworks, accountability measures and legal and regulatory instruments;

- implement whole-of-government and whole-of-society approaches – nationally and locally – to ensure coherence and accountability across policies, programmes and delivery systems in how common equity objectives are set and taken forward.

I am impressed with the work that has gone into this report to start to fill this knowledge gap!

The ideas behind the principles of good governance for the social determinants of health are not entirely new, but, as pointed out in the report, few countries in Europe apply these principles to decision-making in a systematic way. In order to remedy this situation, new skills, partnerships and instruments will be needed, both in countries and throughout WHO, both in Europe and globally.

Beyond the principles and values that characterize Health 2020 lie a real opportunity and challenge: to put them into practice in today's complex societies. European societies invariably frame priorities in terms of economic and fiscal soundness, social cohesion and human development. We must strongly position our health agenda to show that such priorities can be achieved by ensuring the promotion and protection of population health and equity.

This report will be of great value in accompanying us on such a journey!

Zsuzsanna Jakab
Regional Director

AUTHORS

Chris Brown, Programme Manager, WHO European Office for Investment for Health and Development, WHO Regional Office for Europe

Dominic Harrison, Joint Director of Public Health, NHS Blackburn with Darwen, United Kingdom

Erio Ziglio, Head of Office, WHO European Office for Investment for Health and Development, WHO Regional Office for Europe

Harry Burns, Chief Medical Officer for Scotland, The Scottish Government, Edinburgh, Scotland, United Kingdom

ABBREVIATIONS

CIS	Commonwealth of Independent States
COSLA	Convention of Scottish Local Authorities
EU	European Union
GDP	gross domestic product
HTA	health technology assessment
ICESCR	International Covenant on Economic, Social and Cultural Rights
IMF	International Monetary Fund
NAO	United Kingdom's National Audit Office
NCD	noncommunicable disease
NGO	nongovernmental organization
OHCHR	Office of the United Nations High Commissioner for Human Rights
SWAP	sector-wide approach
UNDP	United Nations Development Programme
VIP	Village Investment Project

EXECUTIVE SUMMARY

The majority of countries across the WHO European Region declare improving population health as being among their core goals in national and local policies and plans. Likewise, equity is expressed as a core value (in various ways) in constitutional frameworks and in individual country and European development frameworks and documents. Significant progress has been made to advance improvements in health within and between countries, with average life expectancy for men and women increasing and infant mortality falling. However, these improvements mask the real picture of health in Europe, which shows significant and persistent inequities in avoidable health risks and premature death within all countries, along with gaps between countries across the Region. This also applies between comparable countries.

These health inequities mirror inequities in the material conditions and social and political structures within societies: that is, in the social determinants of health. Consequently, addressing these inequities in health requires joint action by multiple stakeholders and policies that have an influence on the diverse and often complex decision-making processes within these structures.

To better understand and shed light on reasons why good intentions have not translated into improved health outcomes for all, it is necessary to look at policy responses and also at the ways those policy decisions are being made, implemented and reviewed: that is, to explore how well governing for equity in health through action on social determinants is being carried out. This is the central theme of the report. It primarily has a focus on governance systems and capacity within countries, while recognizing that health inequities and governance responses are increasingly influenced by agencies, processes and agendas beyond national borders, in Europe and globally.

Governance is typically used to describe the institutions, rules and norms through which policies are developed and implemented and through which accountability is enforced. However, for the purpose of this report it refers to more than a set of regulations or bureaucratic mechanisms. As the United Nations Educational, Scientific and Cultural Organization state in their 2009 publication *Overcoming inequality: why governance matters (1)*, governance is not just about abstract institutional processes or formal rules. It is also about power relationships in society. At its most basic level, governance systems define who decides on policies, how resources are distributed across society and how governments are held accountable.

Governance to reduce inequities in health through action on social determinants therefore has the overall aim of strengthening the coherence of actions across sectors and stakeholders in a manner which increases resource flows to (a) redress current patterns and magnitude of health inequities; and (b) improve the distribution of determinants in opportunity to be healthy, as well as in risk and consequences of disease and premature mortality, across the population. This implies governance arrangements that are capable of building and ensuring joint action and accountability of health and non-health sectors, public and private actors and of citizens, for a common interest in improving health on equal terms.

This report has been informed by the thinking set out in the report *Governance for health in the 21st century: a study conducted for the WHO Regional Office for Europe (2)*. It primarily draws on information gathered from key informant interviews and a rapid review of official meeting reports and published papers, exploring aspects of practice in governing for social determinants of health and the reduction of health inequities. As such, the report used an enquiry-based research methodology to gather and analyse information.

The report does not seek to prescribe an ideal or "best" governance structure which countries should adopt. Instead it draws out – from the research literature and from operational case study material – a set of general functions that need to be embedded in the governance arrangements of a country in order to deliver improved equity in health through action on social determinants. Recommendations made in the report are therefore generic. This is deliberate and in recognition that further debate and work in this area is needed to enable appropriate adaptation of recommendations to different policy-making levels across diverse cultures, traditions and development conditions within the countries in the WHO European Region.

1.1. Health inequities in Europe

Although overall population health has improved, there are significant differences in health across the WHO European Region, notably a gap in life expectancy of about 16 years between countries (see Fig. 1.1), with even greater differences when account is taken of gender and other inequalities within countries.

Fig. 1.1. Life expectancy (years) for countries in the WHO European Region, 2008 or latest available year

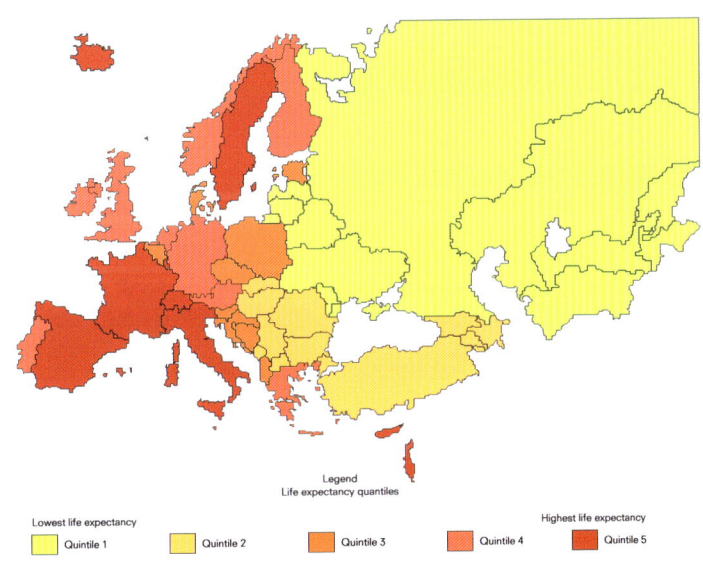

Source: European Health for All database *(3).*

Inequalities in health are therefore a major public health priority within the WHO European Region. A recent review of health indicators for the Region reveals dramatic differences in health and life expectancy. For example, there is a 25-fold difference between the countries

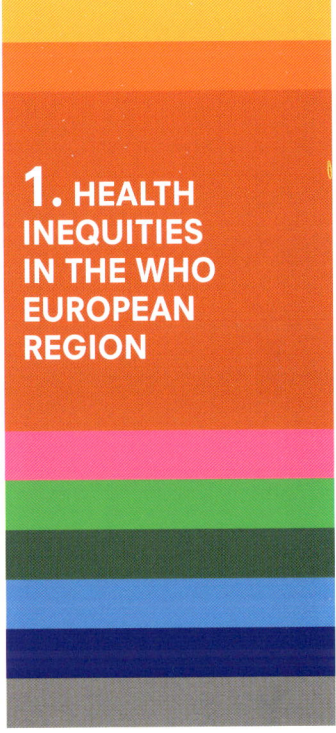

1. HEALTH INEQUITIES IN THE WHO EUROPEAN REGION

GOVERNANCE FOR SOCIAL DETERMINANTS AND HEALTH EQUITY

with the highest and lowest rates of infant mortality. There is also an estimated difference of 30- to 40-fold in maternal mortality ratio between the countries with the highest and lowest rates.

In general, men die younger than women, while women experience more years in poorer health. As Fig. 1.2 shows, the differences between men and women vary widely, with a range of 20 years and 12 years, respectively. Life expectancy for men was about 4–7 years lower than for women in most of the WHO European Region, but 12 years lower than for women in Belarus, Lithuania, the Russian Federation and Ukraine, and 13 years lower in Latvia. In contrast, life expectancy for females was only one year longer than for males in Tajikistan.

Fig. 1.2. Life expectancy (years) at birth by sex for countries in the WHO European Region, 2010 or latest available year

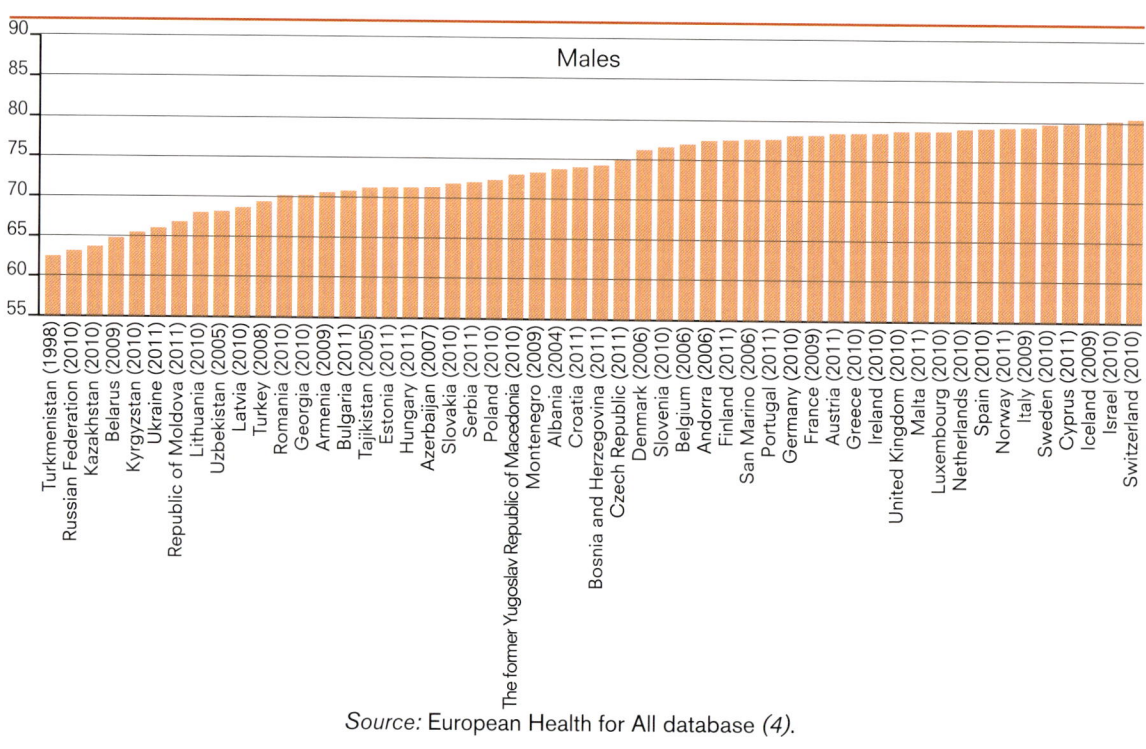

Source: European Health for All database (4).

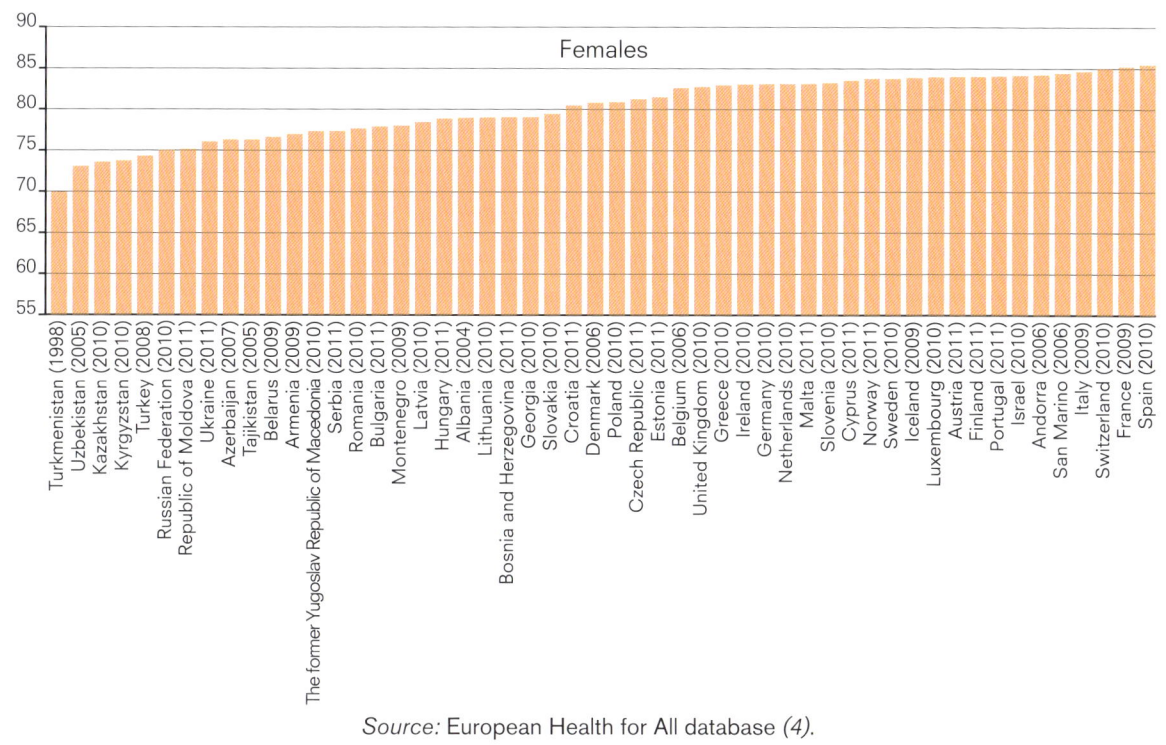

Source: European Health for All database (4).

At the same time there is a marked difference in male and female life expectancy between subregions in Europe. The latest data from the WHO Regional Office for Europe's European Health for All database show that in a 13-year period between 1980 and 2008 the gap in life expectancy in countries of central and eastern Europe compared to those in northern and western Europe rose from 3.7 to 5.4 years for females and for males from 4.3 to 7.3 years. Even between more comparable countries, differences exist (see Fig. 1.3).

Significant gaps in health outcomes exist within countries and are rooted in differences in social status, income, ethnicity, gender and disability. For example, life expectancy for Roma populations in eastern Europe is about 10–15 years less than that for the overall population.

Health inequities in the WHO European Region

In all countries across the WHO European Region, those without education or who leave school early experience worse health over their life course and die younger, compared with those with access to (and who complete) secondary and tertiary education.

Fig. 1.3. Distribution of life years lost, by causes, for member countries of the South-eastern Europe Health Network, 2011

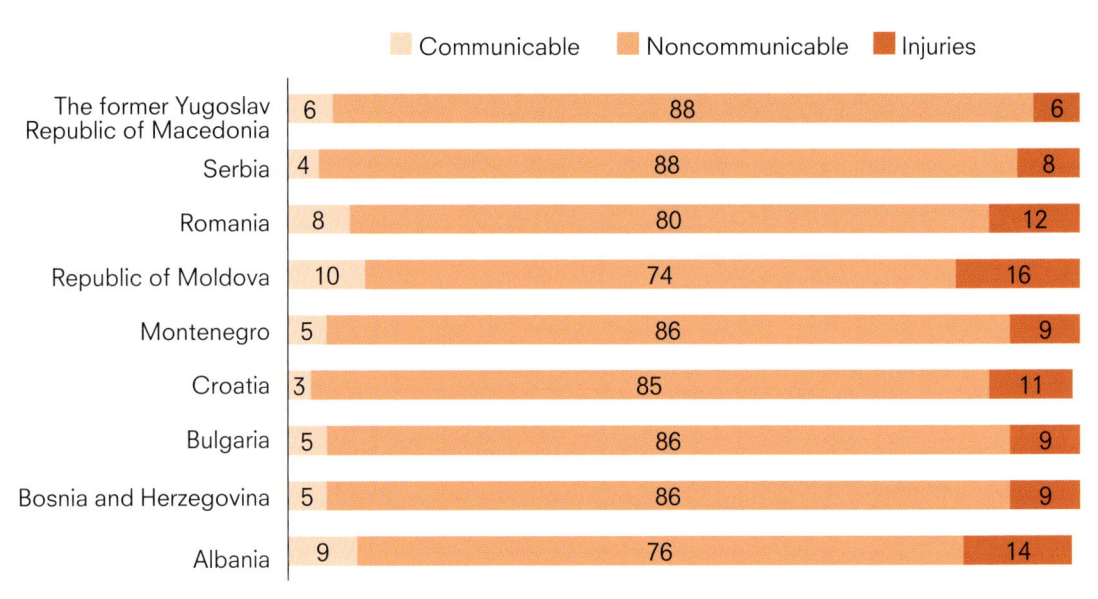

Source: WHO *(5)*.

Risks and burden of noncommunicable diseases (NCDs) in all European countries cluster around the most poor and vulnerable in society. The social and economic differences in health and risk of illness are also seen in countries with higher overall rates of poverty in the population. For example, a recent review of inequalities in NCDs in low- and middle-income countries using 2002–2004 World Health Survey data from 41 countries, including five countries from central Asia and the Caucasus, showed unequal distribution of NCDs, across socioeconomic groups, with prevalence of angina, arthritis, asthma, depression and co-morbidity increasing in line with increasing poverty and low educational level *(6)*.

These data illustrate that for all countries in the WHO European Region, irrespective of development conditions, the opportunity to be healthy and gaps in morbidity and mortality are not the result of genetic or biological conditions but relate to social, economic and political conditions and are therefore largely unnecessary. Most importantly, these discrepancies are amenable to intervention. Strengthening governance and delivery systems to better respond to the challenge will be a critical success factor for reducing avoidable gaps in health within and between countries across the WHO European Region and in pursuit of a fair and sustainable society.

2. TRENDS IN GOVERNANCE THINKING AND PRACTICE

2.1. Reducing inequities in health through action on social determinants – why governance is important

At both global and country levels, a wide range of social, technological, political and cultural factors are making effective governance a more complex task, as the "locus of control" for governance dissipates across societies.

At the global level, there is a trend for governments to cede national control and sovereignty to international trade agreements, multinational companies and wider legislative frameworks established on the basis of (quasi-) political and legislative unions, such as with the European Union (EU). This highlights how national policy commitment to equity in health and social determinants of health is increasingly shaped by factors and agencies beyond local and national borders. These include external bodies that influence national policy priorities and commitment; for example, United Nations agencies, the EU, the development banks, and unilateral and multilateral donors and foundations, such as the Open Society Foundation and Ashoka.

Some of these influences can be positive for sustaining a health equity agenda and increasing understanding of or support for acting on social determinants and their distribution in society. They can give political weight to the issue in national and local decision-making by incentivizing commitment. Examples include use of the open method of coordination by the EU in relation to, for example, Roma integration and the social protection and social inclusion agenda. Also influential is the use of common development frameworks and integrated "sector-wide approaches" (SWAPs), which explicitly include measures of equity in monitoring development assistance to incentivize coherent action across sectors and agencies as part of poverty reduction strategies.

Many influences from beyond national borders can also have unintended negative consequences in terms of the social determinants of health. For example, some relevant grey literature[1] highlighted that the International Monetary Fund (IMF) loans criteria were

---

[1] Unpublished background paper for the WHO Regional Office for Europe review of the social determinants of health; 2012. See also the Bibliography section.

adversely restricting the flexibilities of lower-income economies and those in transition, to stimulate investment in public goods (such as employment and social protection), compared to countries that are better off, both in Europe and globally.

These trends and examples highlight the increasing connection between domestic and foreign decision-making processes and their impact(s) on social determinants. In the report, *Governance for health in the 21st century: a study conducted for the WHO Regional Office for Europe (2)*, Kickbusch et al. argue how decisions and impacts are increasingly interdependent and complex and identifies where solutions need to be jointly produced. This is highly relevant to governance for health equity, whereby many of the factors that shape the patterns and magnitude of health inequities within a country – including nature and type of employment, housing and environmental conditions, income level and security, education and community resources – lie beyond the direct control of ministries of health. The manner in which these factors are distributed in a given society can be positively influenced by ministries of health and the actions of other sectors, including within government, and other stakeholders (public and private) who shape decision-making processes and outcomes. In this way, health equity should be pursued as a product of the actions of multiple stakeholders, shaped by decisions made in many different arenas of government, and corporate and public life.

Increasingly, the wider literature and practices dealing with governance for equitable outcomes (and specifically the field of health) highlight the need for increased involvement of local people and communities in defining problems and generating/implementing solutions. There are two main reasons why this is an important aspect of governing for equity in health through action on social determinants. First, in transition economies (most commonly, but not only in these), as state health systems liberalize there is an increase in private health care provision, often characterized by inadequately regulated profit-making providers. If in these contexts the capacity and mechanisms for regulation, guidance and enforcement are weak, providers are not driven to consider need, but rather the ability of the patient to pay. Common results include rising costs of basic health and medical care and profit-driven criteria for access and availability of services *(7)*. The impact is borne by the whole of society, but with more catastrophic effects on those that are resource poor, who delay seeking medical help, and pay proportionately more of their household income for treatment and care. Studies show how these health impacts are not only bad for those affected and for the performance of the health sector; they also have both direct and indirect knock-on effects on the achievements of poverty reduction strategies by lowering human development potential. The costs therefore also fall on development ministries, government and the community of international donors. In this way health equity impacts are the responsibility of all stakeholders in society *(7—9)*.[2]

Across western, central and eastern Europe there are several examples of previously state-commissioned and state-provided health services being deregulated, liberalizing and privatizing part or all of the provision of health care as part of health reforms. The consumption of health services as a "consumer good" – differentially accessed on the basis of ability to pay – will likely generate increased health inequity across Europe. In these circumstances, joint systems of governance between citizens and the state are essential if avoidable deaths and increased costs associated with preventable mortality are to be avoided.

A second reason why involving local people and stakeholders is important in governing for equity in health stems from studies evaluating country experiences of implementing inequity reduction policies strategies and programmes. These indicate a need to place more emphasis on local solutions to tackle stubborn patterns of inequities, including those associated with health. Interviews with policy-makers about approaches to policy development in countries across Europe suggest that when policies are being designed there is often a lack of understanding of the social, cultural and economic lives of the resource poor population. The result is interventions which are often mismatched to the realities of people's lives and can fall short of delivering intended benefits for those most in need. In some cases the consequences are to unintentionally benefit some groups more than others, thus widening gaps in health within countries.

---

[2] A resource guide on governance for social determinants of health and health inequities is also in preparation at the WHO Regional Office for Europe's European Office for Investment for Health and Development.

For these two reasons, governing for equity needs to be improved by developing new and/or strengthened instruments and mechanisms that engage the intended beneficiaries of policies in decision-making processes. Specifically, emphasis should be placed on ensuring that the differential needs of marginalized and at-risk groups are recognized, and that they are involved in resource allocations, and the design, monitoring and review of policies, services and interventions. In doing so, health equity governance could also contribute to promoting and supporting social inclusion and social justice in society(ies).

Against this backdrop, governance for health equity has an important role to play in order to:

- develop the necessary legislation and regulations to strengthen **joint accountability for equity**, across sectors and decision-makers and within and outside of government;

- use mechanisms which actively promote **involvement of local people** and stakeholders in problem definition and solution development;

- ensure **regular joint review of progress**, which fosters common understanding and sustains commitment to deliver shared results over time;

- draw on **different forms of evidence** to ensure policies address the main causal pathways and are capable of adapting over time.

Kickbusch et al. (2) describe these points as (some of the) features of smart governance for health in the 21st century. At the core of this concept is recognition that complex issues – such as problems that have no simple solution or to which the solution cannot be found through research alone (for example, issues surrounding inequities) – require new system-based governance approaches. Such approaches are capable of addressing the interdependencies of factors (determinants, stakeholders, settings) that are part of the causal chain and necessary for achieving sustainable solutions.

This highlights the extent to which governance is important, not only in terms of preventing and mitigating the effects of actions which are likely to produce inequity in health, but also in terms of opportunity to position and sustain health and health equity as important assets which contribute to the attainment of other societal goals and values. This is because many of the determinants of health equity/inequity are also shared priorities for other sectors and government and society. This includes goals such as social inclusion/cohesion, poverty reduction, sustainable development and community resilience, that is, the ability of communities to successfully manage social, economic and environmental "shocks". These goals provide a convergence point for common action across sectors, which – if due attention to their distribution is given – will produce benefits for many sectors including for health and health equity.

For these reasons, key goals in governing for equity in health through action on social determinants include:

- creating and sustaining political **support for (health) equity as a societal good**;

- strengthening the coherence of actions across sectors (policies, investments, services) and stakeholders (public, private, and voluntary), which increases resource flows to redress the current patterns and magnitude of health inequity;

- improving the distribution of the determinants of opportunities to be healthy, across the whole population.

This highlights how health inequities are just one outcome of inequity. Other areas of inequity include inequities in life opportunities, education, income, housing, transport, water and sanitation, and so on – each of which is part of the causal pathways known to lead to inequity in health. Governing for equity in health therefore involves a commitment, not only to a value of health but also to the concept of "equity in all policies". This is a means of achieving mutual benefits that accrue to multiple sectors as well as a public good that produces benefits for the whole of society *(10)*.

The wider literature dealing with why it is important to aim to reduce inequities through action on social determinants highlights many compelling reasons. A rapid review of published and unpublished meeting reports and national strategy documents for countries across Europe shows one or a combination of these reasons are evident. The following section summarizes the reasons that are most commonly mentioned or cited as being fundamental by Member States across the WHO European Region.

2.2. Reasons for acting on social determinants and reducing health inequities

2.2.1. Reducing preventable ill health is a matter of fairness and social justice

Across Europe, many people die prematurely each year as a result of health inequity. In England, for instance, 2.5 million years of life are potentially lost to health inequity by those dying prematurely each year. In Slovakia, the infant and adult mortality rates in poorer regions is almost twice that of most developed regions *(11)*. In the Netherlands, mortality and morbidity in the population would be reduced by 25–50% if men with fewer years in education had the same mortality and morbidity levels as those with university education. In these and all countries across the WHO European Region, the unfair distribution of health, well-being and life expectancy means that people with fewer social and economic resources have reduced life chances and their opportunities to lead a flourishing life are unnecessarily curtailed.

The extent to which inequalities may be counterbalanced in a society or community relies on a sense of what constitutes social justice, human rights and equality.

2.2.2. Health is a human right

Health is a human right, indispensable in fulfilling the fundamental human rights principle that human dignity is inviolable. It has been recognized as such in many international treaties and conventions, as has the impact of other human rights on health. Examples of such conventions include the 1946 WHO Constitution *(12)*, the 1948 Universal Declaration of Human Rights *(13)*, and the 1966 International Covenant on Economic, Social and Cultural Rights (ICESCR) *(14)* – a legally binding instrument of international law.

Almost every country has ratified at least one international human rights treaty recognizing the right to health. The right to health is referred to in 115 constitutions and covers the right to accessible, available, adequate-quality health care. It also includes a wide range of factors that can lead to a healthy life, including the protection of health. They include:

- safe drinking-water and adequate sanitation
- safe food
- adequate nutrition and housing
- healthy working and environmental conditions
- health-related education and information
- gender equity.

As defined by the Office of the United Nations High Commissioner for Human Rights (OHCHR) and WHO, the right to health embodies a set of unalienable freedoms and entitlements. These include, for example:

- the right to a system of health protection, providing equality of opportunity for everyone to enjoy the highest attainable level of health;
- the right to prevention, treatment and control of diseases;
- access to essential medicines;
- maternal, child and reproductive health.

Health as a human right therefore defines both a legal obligation and a set of values that are applied in a human rights-based approach to local, national and global health (2). At the population level, new sources of health information, expanding transnational telecommunications capacities and changes in where and how people seek information are contributing to the democratization of knowledge, including knowledge about health and its determinants. This transition to so-called more open societies has increased pressure for greater transparency and accountability in decision-making within governments. It has also shifted the locus of control in governing for health and fair outcomes to a much wider range of stakeholders – without the participation of which, governance cannot be effectively exercised. It is worth noting that, across and within countries, democratization of knowledge for health and of health itself as part of transition to open societies is taking place at different rates.

Thus, there is an ongoing need for instruments and agencies at local, national and European levels, to protect and promote the right to health, including knowledge of and participation in decision-making processes. This involves ensuring that different groups in the population are able to exercise their rights to obtain and use information, as well as holding others to account for decisions and their impacts. Across Europe, this includes legitimizing and strengthening the role of ombudsmen, engaging and working with the OHCHR, formally recognizing (for example, through laws) the role of independent agencies, nongovernmental organizations (NGOs) and civil society groups, and establishing pan-European bodies which protect and promote human rights (such as the European human rights agency, Freedom House).

In addition to this, the role of government in governance remains critical and is in fact expanding in many areas of modern life. This change in role might be characterized by defining government as the "conductor" of governance systems, rather than being the orchestra itself.

Research indicates the need for a combination of governance approaches – using a mix of hard and soft instruments, for example laws, regulations and dialogue, consultations and joint sectoral/stakeholder reviews – for the benefit of health and well-being. These approaches, when combined, are most effective in governing for complex issues.

Trends in governance thinking and practice

2.2.3. Health is a public good

Health is both a public good and a national asset. Public goods are entities, such as peace and security, law and order, street signs and traffic rules – capacities of communities that are in the public domain. If they are adequately provided, everyone can benefit from these goods; if they are underprovided – where, for example, law and order suffer and crime and violence prevails – society as a whole suffers. Health is a key asset of individuals, communities and nations, contributing directly to well-being in society and indirectly to other public goods, such as increased social cohesion and human development potential.

2.2.4. Loss of health and increasing health inequity lead to social conflict and undermines community cohesion

Health inequities deny communities access to equal life chances in terms of life expectancy, income, housing and so on, which in turn affect individual and community capacities to meet basic human needs. Competition for resources that are necessary for a healthy life – such as energy, water, food, shelter and employment – is increasingly becoming a cause of conflict both within and between countries. Securing "fair share" access to these resources is essential for both peace and community cohesion *(15)*. This thinking reflects a significant body of new knowledge about the complex interrelationship between health and sustainable human development. The health of populations and the determinants of health equity are critical for social coherence and economic growth, and are a vital resource for human development *(16)*.

This link between inequity, social instability and development is reinforced by the United Nations Development Programme (UNDP) in the report *Towards human resilience: sustaining MDG progress in an age of uncertainty (17)*, which states: "High [income] inequality is associated with higher crime rates, lower life expectancy and conflict".

2.2.5. Population health is an economic asset and a productive good

A high level of population health is an economic asset. Conversely, the economic consequences of avoidable illness constitute a major burden on the individuals concerned, and on economic development capacity and labour market productivity. Many studies show how shortfalls in health are associated with low economic productivity and reduced quality of life *(2)*. For instance, due to ill health in the United Kingdom some 175 million working days are lost each year, costing the economy £100 billion in lost productivity, benefits and taxes *(18)*. Similar calculations of losses to labour market productivity from avoidable ill health and pockets of entrenched poor health among the population have been calculated for other countries and have been the subject of several major multi-country reports (for example Suhrcke, Rocco & McKee *(19)* and the forthcoming volume edited by McDaid, Sassi & Merkur, entitled *The economic case for public health action (20)*.

There is growing interest in health as a productive good. Across Europe, health care costs are escalating and there is growing evidence of poor allocative efficiency of health care system spending.[3] This is because health and social care system resources still in many instances cluster around curative or acute services, at great cost, neglecting the potential of primary prevention and health promotion to prevent up to 70% of the disease burden in European countries. An international rapid review (in 2006) of the societal costs of potentially preventable illnesses concluded that a 10% improvement in outcomes as a result of prevention, education and social marketing could save families £7 billion, reduce public expenditure by £3 billion, reduce employer costs by £1.5 billion and generate returns to society worth over £8 billion *(21)*. This study, as with many others, highlights the economic value of a healthier society, as a resource (and asset) for social and economic development.

---

[3] Allocative efficiency occurs when there is an optimal distribution of goods and services. It is often contrasted with technical efficiency, which is the effectiveness with which a given set of inputs is used to produce an output [author's own definition].

Given that the risks and burden of preventable disease and co-morbidity of NCDs in all European countries cluster around the most poor and vulnerable in society, the human and societal costs are magnified. This signals the need for interventions to focus on reducing the burden of disease across the whole population, but with efforts intensified for those experiencing or at risk of social and economic exclusion.

Without action, avoidable health costs (to governments, institutions and individuals) will escalate. Calculations of the costs of not acting to reduce inequities in health are already well documented. Recent studies relevant to high- and middle-income countries in the EU show that inequality-related losses to health amount to more than 700 000 deaths per year and 33 million prevalent cases of ill health in the EU community as a whole. These losses account for 20% of the total costs of health care and 15% of the total costs of social security benefits. Inequality-related losses to health reduce labour productivity and reduce gross domestic product (GDP) by 1.4% each year. The monetary value of health inequity-related welfare losses is estimated to be €980 billion per year or 9.4% of GDP. Inequity costs are not restricted to wealthier countries but are also mirrored in lower income and transition economies *(18)*.

2.3. Summary of key issues in governance for health equity

The previous section highlights the challenges and imperatives involved in tackling social determinants of health to reduce health inequities. This has highlighted the importance of separating the notion of **governance of health** from the wider concept of **governance for health**. This is because governance **of** health usually refers to actions by and directed towards the health care system; namely, its policy, expenditure and decision-making.

Conversely, governance **for** health refers to the governance of health outcomes (both intended and unintended) relating to policy, expenditure and decision-making across the whole of government and society (that is, in the non-health sphere as well as in the health sector). This report argues that reducing inequities through action on social determinants needs to be embedded in an approach which governs **for** health, which is a broader concept than the governance **of** health. Inferences drawn from research suggest this reflects new understanding about health in society. The key points about governance **for** health are summarized in Box 2.1.

> **Box 2.1. Governance for health**
>
> 1. "Governance for health and well-being" is a central building block of good governance. It is guided by a value framework which includes health as: a human right; a global public good; a component of well-being; and a matter of social justice.
>
> 2. The expanded understanding of health includes considering health as an emergent property of many societal systems – it therefore requires action in many systems, sometimes with and sometimes without the involvement of the health sector.
>
> 3. Whole-of-government and whole-of-society approaches reflect this reality and are grounded in strategies which enhance joined-up government, improved coordination and integration, and diffusion of responsibility for health throughout government and society.
>
> 4. "Governance for health" builds on the experiences gained in the health arena with intersectoral action, healthy public policy and "health in all policies".
>
> 5. The actions needed to improve health and reduce health inequities require new systems-based governance and delivery mechanisms that take account of interdependencies, complexity and the need for whole-of-government and whole-of-society co-production of population health.
>
> 6. New governance and delivery systems capable of producing improvements in social determinants of health are multi-layered and multi-dimensional. These require increasing empowerment of local citizens to create shared health value.
>
> 7. Health is increasingly recognized as a critical economic and social asset, the realization of which can add value to existing economic investments, business efficiency, effectiveness and performance.
>
> 8. Government has a critical role in determining the conditions through which health governance and delivery of improvements in the social determinants of health and health equity are achieved.

These new understandings about how health is produced and valued – along with related implications for governance – highlight common features of more effective systems of governing for health equity through action on social determinants. Kickbusch et al. *(2)* summarize the following characteristics of smart governance:

1. governing through collaboration
2. governing through citizen engagement
3. governing through a mix of regulation and persuasion
4. governing through independent agencies and expert bodies
5. governing through adaptive policies, resilient structures and foresight.

"Smart governance for health" therefore embodies a combination of these characteristics in the strategic approach to addressing health challenges, including reducing inequities in health as whole-of-government and whole-of-society approaches.

2.4. Summary of the main principles of effective governance for health equity

A large part of the following section on governance is taken directly from the 2011 report entitled *Governance for health in the 21st century: a study conducted for the WHO Regional Office for Europe (2)*. Based on a review of case studies looking at new approaches to governance for health, Kickbusch proposes five types of **"smart governance for health"**, listed here, which should be considered and combined when embarking on whole-of-government and whole-of-society approaches.

1. **Governing through collaboration is the new imperative.** Kickbusch et al. argue that key lessons can be learned from the rich literature available on collaborative governance, including that due consideration should be given to (a) the process and design of collaboration; (b) the virtuous cycle between communication, trust, commitment and understanding; (c) the choice of tools and mechanisms available; and (d) the need for transparency and accountability.

2. **As to governing through citizen engagement, public policy can no longer just be delivered.** Successful "governance for health" requires joint production, as well as the involvement and cooperation of citizens, consumers and patients. As governance becomes more diffused throughout society, working directly with the public can help to ensure that transparency and accountability are strengthened. Partnering with and empowering the public are also crucial to ensuring that values are upheld. Technology – especially smart phones and networked social media – is a driving force that enables citizens, as well as changing the ways governments and health systems can do business, for example through eHealth. Within these new, complex relationships between state and society, participation, transparency and accountability become engines for innovation.

3. **Governing is becoming more fluid, multi-level, multi-stakeholder and adaptive in nature.** Traditional hierarchical means of governance are increasingly complemented by other mechanisms, such as soft power and soft law.[4] This includes self-regulation, governance by persuasion, alliances, networks and open methods of coordination, as well as the new role of citizens in monitory democracy.[5] At the same time, hierarchical multi-level regulations that extend from the global to the local levels (such as many EU regulations) are becoming more common and impacting on many dimensions of individuals' lifestyles, behaviour and daily life.

4. **To govern through new independent agencies and expert bodies, evidence is critical in a knowledge-based society.** The study finds that (as in other fields of governance) independent expert bodies, such as federal agencies, commissions, regulators and auditors are playing an increasingly vital role in providing evidence, monitoring ethical boundaries, expanding accountability and strengthening democratic governance for health, as related to privacy, risk assessment, quality control or health technology assessment (HTA) and health impact assessment. The importance of these entities increases as countries make

---

[4] Soft power – in general terms – means exercising power through influence, while soft law means exercising power through setting social/normative expectations.
[5] Monitory democracy means achieving democracy by monitoring methods, for example, by making public and civic data accessible and transparent.

Trends in governance thinking and practice

the transition to a knowledge-based society that is more readily innovative. The literature indicates that it is also important to improve metrics (that is, figures that can meaningfully indicate what is being assessed) – for example, to include both objective and subjective measures – in order to capture what is happening across the population, requiring a mix of aggregate and disaggregate data.

5. **Governing through adaptive policies, resilient structures and foresight is needed because there is no simple causality or solution to complex issues.** The study finds that whole-of-government and whole-of-society approaches to health need to be capable of managing complex factors affecting health and to respond in real time, or even ahead of time; that is, to be adaptive and to mirror the characteristics of complexity. The latter may include decentralized decision-making, and self-organizing/social networking should be enabled to ensure stakeholders can respond quickly to unanticipated events in innovative ways. Interventions should be iterative and designed to focus on learning and adaptation from knowledge gathered and shared with multiple stakeholders. In this way policy implementation is seen as an ongoing process of review and adjustment, capable of identifying and addressing how interventions in one area can have unintended consequences in another. These are features of what the study calls "anticipatory governance".

Given the long-term nature of many health problems, new forecasting methodologies are considered to be important as part of effective governance. This includes the use of futures modelling and scenario-based policy analysis, sometimes referred to as foresight mechanisms. These serve to assess how the causal pathways leading to inequities in health may be influenced by emerging social, economic, political and cultural trends in society. Their value lies in allowing decision-makers to react more quickly and adapt to changes which may affect the attainment of policy priorities. These techniques can also boost societal resilience by shifting policy focus away from risks to address more fundamental systemic challenges, as well as deliberating jointly the "social" (that is, values-related) and the "science" (that is, evidence-related) aspects of public policy. In this way they may also lead to innovations in addressing complex health problems and to sustaining policy action over time.

Across the WHO European Region there is increased interest in and action towards developing and implementing whole-of-government and whole-of-society approaches which embody some or many of the aforementioned features of effective governance. Boxes 2.2 and 2.3 provide examples to illustrate this in practice.

> **Box 2.2. Example of a whole-of-government approach to social inclusion in Poland**
>
> The social inclusion strategy led by Poland's Ministry of Labour and Social Policy – reporting directly to the Prime Minister's office – was a highly collaborative policy development process across government and involving NGOs, community-based organizations and regional and municipal stakeholders and organizations. The process lasted 18 months and involved joint review of current and past policies and data on the impact of and trends in social inclusion. Appraisal of promising practices from across Europe – using participatory methods, including stakeholder fora and roundtable events – helped to stimulate debate and inform available options, building on the perspectives of different stakeholders. Major efforts were made to promote informal meetings and discussions, with the aim of better understanding and exploring how social inclusion was viewed and could be better included in government policies and decision-making processes (budgets, reporting, resource allocation and local action). This mix of formal and informal mechanisms across levels of government and stakeholders illustrates the components of "smart governance" for building a whole-of-government approach to improving social inclusion in Poland. Further incentives exist in the form of opportunities to access funding through the EU Structural Funds mechanism, by means of compliance with the EU Cohesion Policy.

More widely, the same characteristics are evident in practice with regard to the attainment of other strategic goals, such as social inclusion, poverty reduction, and sustainable development. Across Europe, some or all of the five characteristics of smart governance for health can be seen or are embedded in mainstream governance practice for health equity and for public policies that have significant impact on social determinants and (health) equity.

Trends in governance thinking and practice

Box 2.3. Example of a whole-of-government and whole-of-society approach to reducing inequities in Scotland

In Scotland, concerns about the poor indicators of social and economic progress and the related shortfall in human development potential across society was the impetus for a whole-of-government approach to reducing inequities, under the national framework entitled "Scotland Performs". Addressing the costs to society of poor health and inequities in health between social groups was articulated as being important to the attainment of Scotland Performs. This resulted in the development of the "Equally Well" framework. A Ministerial Task Force was established with clear terms of reference to guide their work. The Task Force reported to the First Minister (Scotland's equivalent of a Prime Minister) and worked for 12 months to review evidence, model policy options and debate priorities for action. Methods used included expert panels, seminars and public consultations to ensure the involvement of a wide range of stakeholders from national and local authorities, NGOs, academia, business, and public service providers.

This ensured many perspectives and areas of expertise were used to inform policy options and in the generation (testing) of solutions. Once priorities were formulated, a review of delivery capacity and systems was carried out to ensure that the goals could be achieved successfully. This served to identify where delivery systems needed to be strengthened and/or adjusted prior to launching the Equally Well framework. Implementation has been under way since 2007 and includes formal agreements and an accountability framework for action between national and local levels (such as the concordat with the Convention of Scottish Local Authorities (COSLA), which is a formal agreement on priorities, responsibilities and the relationship between the national and local levels *(22)*.

A clear joint process for review and ongoing assessment has been established. A principal instrument used is the Single Outcome Agreements. These are agreements between the Scottish Government and local-level planning units called community planning partnerships. They set out how the Scottish Government and local-level planning teams will work towards improving outcomes for local people in a way that reflects local circumstances and priorities.

Regular public reports and debates on progress are also undertaken, along with independent reviews to inform policy adaptation over time. An important feature of this approach was the introduction of test sites, which allow policy to be tested in a structured way, with the aim of informing the scaling up of effective actions to tackle critical problems. Capacity building for public sector staff and other partners is ongoing, in order to ensure policy is mainstreamed across government and to strengthen human resource capacity to reduce inequities in Scotland.

The discussion in Chapter 3 highlights the importance of governance for reducing inequities and shows promising developments. It emphasizes the need to engage multiple stakeholders, to use a variety of instruments to incentivize collaboration across stakeholders and to hold decision-makers to account for decisions and their impacts. Participation of local people and the intended beneficiaries of policies are underlined as being important to improving not only the transparency of decisions but also the efficacy of actions (policies/investments) to improve equity in health through action on social determinants.

3.1. Integrated policies capable of acting on social determinants

Across Europe, the developments set out in this chapter are being reflected to a greater or lesser extent in local, regional and national governance arrangements. A review of European country experiences and formal documents shows that there is an increased recognition of the need to develop integrated policies and solutions which can act on underlying determinants of health and health equity. These include comprehensive health inequity reduction strategies covering the whole population and spectrum of determinants, such as those found in Norway and Scotland. More common are issue-specific programmes and policies aimed at certain target groups; these can be found in almost all countries across the WHO European Region. Examples to illustrate this are the Roma inclusion strategies in place in the countries of central, southern and eastern Europe. A further focus for integrated policies is the inclusion of health improvement goals and objectives in national poverty reduction strategies, such as those that can be found in many of the Commonwealth of Independent States (CIS) countries. The indicators to measure improvements in health between different groups across the population are often generic and equity is more commonly implicit than explicit (that is, a value rather than a performance criteria for integrated action). This may reflect, as Gwatkin suggests *(9)*, that health inequity and other distributional aspects of health status and service have enjoyed varying degrees of attention as measures of development in lower income countries (and in the development community) over the years:

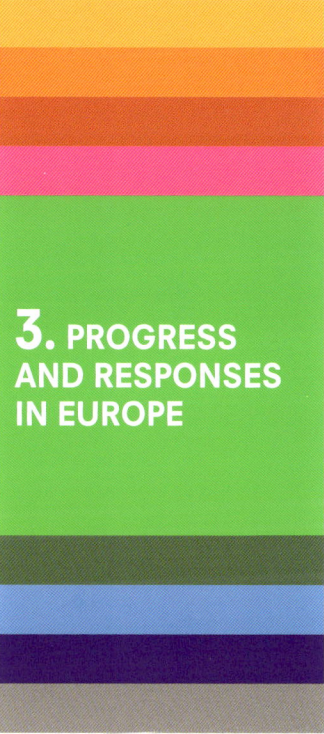

3. PROGRESS AND RESPONSES IN EUROPE

During the 1970s and early 1980s, distributional concerns (i.e. a concern for the health status of different socioeconomic groups within society as distinct from the overall societal average) were dominant in thought about international health. These concerns then receded for about a decade, from around the mid-1980s to the mid-1990s, as attention turned from equity to efficiency. Now, the pendulum has begun to swing back, and distributional concerns are on the rise.

A fourth approach is to include specific health equity targets in national development plans, such as in the case of Latvia or Slovenia, where in the last few years national and local approaches to tackling inequities have been scaled up. In these cases Ministry of Health is pursuing common equity goals with other sectors, using health equity measures as one of the indicators for joint policy success to increase the equity of public policies.

3.2. Instruments that incentivize collaboration across stakeholders and hold decision-makers to account

Instruments that commonly feature as part of country "tool kits" when governing for integrated policies and to improve distributional (equity) impacts, include the widespread use of impact assessment methodologies, guidance and regulatory bodies and specialist impact assessment units such as those in place in Romania. Other instruments that incentivize cooperation across policy sectors include regular cross-sectoral spending reviews on inequalities (England)[6] and analyses of who benefits from various policies (benefit incidence analysis techniques, such as those used in Serbia within the national Roma inclusion strategy). Increasingly, governance instruments such as these are used by joint working groups and teams involving multiple policy sectors and, in some cases, NGOs and independent academic and policy support units, for example in the Scottish Equally Well framework and in the former Yugoslav Republic of Macedonia's Roma Action Plan (part of the "Decade of Roma Inclusion 2005–2015").

Across the WHO European Regions these developments in accounting jointly for the

---

[6] This was an instrument used by the former government over the 10-year period spanning the life of the national health inequalities strategy *(23)*.

GOVERNANCE FOR HEALTH EQUITY

impact of various actions vary in terms of how systematically they are both used and acted upon. While acknowledged as being necessary to address social determinants and reduce health inequity, cooperative working methods and performance management have also been found to be time consuming, incur significant opportunity costs (loss of personal/sectoral influence, resources and status) and in some cases are contrary to the cultural norms and values that prevail. For these reasons, joint and "softer" instruments need to be combined with more hierarchical or so called "hard" instruments to ensure joint production and joint accountability for equity across different policy domains. These include laws and regulation, parliamentary resolutions, formal memoranda of understandings (including concordats and contracts) and financial and reward systems linked to team results (for example pooled/shared budgets).

Many countries within the WHO European Region are currently reviewing their national and local development plans, as well as evaluating or reforming health policies and services. In many of these there is a direct intention (or an expressed interest) to strengthen accountability mechanisms with the aim of incentivizing actions on social determinants. For example, in 2011 a new Public Health Act was passed in Norway (in effect from 1 January 2012), "to contribute to societal development that promotes public health and reduces social inequities in health" *(24)*. One of the main features of the Norwegian Public Health Act is that it specifies public health work as being a whole-of-government and a whole-of-municipality responsibility, rather than a responsibility of the health sector alone. The law stipulates that Norwegian municipalities must involve all sectors in the promotion of public health, not just the health sector. Additional tools, such as a national system of providing public health indicators to local governments (including indicators of social determinants of health) complement the new law and support action by many stakeholders at different levels of government to execute their responsibilities with the aim of reducing social inequities.

Along similar lines, Kyrgyzstan has elaborated and implemented an Intersectoral Action Plan for Promoting Population Health within the framework of the Manas Taalimi health care reform process. The plan was formally adopted by Parliament following its inclusion in the Law on Health Care Reform (2006), and its implementation is ongoing. This requires coordination of action between health and other sectors to improve daily living conditions, such as water supply and housing, to prevent hygiene-related diseases, improve health behaviours and increase access to primary care services. The Action Plan also serves as a framework to coordinate support from bilateral and unilateral agencies around common objectives for improving health for all at the community level.

3.2.1. Horizontal and vertical integration of actions

Decentralization of responsibilities and thus accountability for the outcome of policy is a strong feature of governance systems in Europe. Increasingly the subnational levels (county, *oblast*, region) have greater autonomy in relation to social and economic decisions and investments, many of which relate to the social determinants of health and health equity, for example housing, environment, water and sanitation, community safety, urban and rural development, including employment and business development. At the same time, health remains a predominantly centrally managed and organized function. This creates challenges and opportunities for ensuring that health and equity are considered in subnational-level policy-making and investment frameworks. Examples such as those from Murska Sobota in Slovenia and Košice in Slovakia illustrate opportunities and responses in Europe. In Košice, the largest self-governing region in the south-eastern part of Slovakia, the regional parliament formally adopted a health chapter into its regional development plan in 2009. Goals for addressing the determinants of health of those with fewer social and economic resources and with poorest health status have been included as a matter of priority across sectors. Implementation actions are reflected in regional investment frameworks and funding flows. While mechanisms used to advance such work are mainly formal and embedded in core planning, accounting and monitoring systems at the regional level, the process was coordinated by a multi-stakeholder group including the Regional Public Health Institute in Košice, the Chair of the Košice Self-governing Region, researchers working on social and economic inequities, regional authority staff working as demographers and as community outreach service providers. This was a powerful combination of stakeholders who were able to access diverse data, discuss ideas and identify challenges through informal access to various stakeholders within and outside of government. A key factor was engaging and drawing on other local knowledge of communities and the intended beneficiaries of the policy to shape the priorities for action. A principal feature of the approach was to engage external agencies to broker dialogue between stakeholders in support of using best available evidence and practice from across Europe and internationally. Specifically, this involved WHO collaborating centres and centres of excellence with expertise in social determinants and cross-sectoral investment for health and equity.

3.3. Active participation and engagement of communities

There is increasing interest in developing partnerships to address the root causes of health inequity, based on bottom-up planning and drawing knowledge from communities to inform interventions and assess policies. Examples which embody these goals and are part of the formal institutional arrangements within countries include the Community Health Partnership in Florence; the Finnish municipality health promotion management groups; the health and well-being boards in England and the World-Bank-supported Village Investment Project (VIP) in Kyrgyzstan. In the latter the aim is to strengthen local capacity and infrastructure for social and economic development in rural areas and to alleviate poverty. In Kyrgyzstan, 65% of the 5.1 million population live in rural areas, and the rural population accounts for about 80% of the extremely poor. The VIP promotes good governance at the level closest to local people, providing the impetus for sustained economic development, and contributing to employment generation in rural areas. Mechanisms that foster participation and ensure transparency in decision-making about priority setting, resource allocation and review include: open public budgeting and planning meetings, community hearings to support participation and capacity building for local people and community organizations in budgeting and participatory planning and implementation activities.

The aforementioned mechanisms illustrate increasing awareness of the assets that local people bring to solving complex problems and the value and importance of genuine and systematic participation in the generation, implementation and review of solutions. Many studies support this development, highlighting how local people may identify problems long before they reach the public policy agenda, as illustrated by the example in Box 3.1.[7]

> **Box 3.1. Children labelling dangerous places and practices in Corker Hill, Scotland**
>
> Routine data systems frequently categorize unintentional injuries to children as being deficits in the child – for example, when injury occurs crossing the road in the wrong kind of way ("ran out without looking"; "didn't use the crossing") or in the parent ("inadequate supervision"). In a study which turned the accidental injury story on its head, by asking not why so many children are injured or die in accidents, but why so many make it to adulthood in unsafe environments, children were encouraged to label places and practices they identified as risky with a skull and crossbones. These are different types of data, but they demonstrate the ability of local communities to spot dangers before they translate into deaths – illustrated by press reports with messages such as "it took a death to persuade the authorities that we really did need a crossing" *(25)*.

Such examples highlight the value of engaging local people in dialogue and participation in identifying and solving problems. Numerous studies show that this contributes to building community ownership and capacity to take control of factors determining their health, as well as better informing the resources and decisions of formal authorities responsible for improving health and determinants *(26)*. These processes, while designed to improve health outcomes, also contribute to building trust in communities and local authorities, increasing transparency in decision-making. These important assets for health and social development will only be effective and sustained if they are part of wider interventions and policies designed to act on the structural determinants of health and as part of mainstream governance practice, rather than one-off projects.

---

[7] A resource guide on governance for social determinants of health and health inequities is in preparation at the WHO Regional Office for Europe's European Office for Investment for Health and Development. Further (grey) literature also informs the background research for this report. For details see the Bibliography.

The report so far has highlighted how the values of equity in health and their attainment are included in diverse ways in European and national policies, frameworks and initiatives. Examples across countries include social inclusion, poverty reduction, balanced development, rural development, universal social and health protection, sustainable communities, and the right to health. All of these have the aim of improving the daily living conditions, working life, income opportunities and safety/security of the population. In this way the social determinants of health and equity are observed in almost all the current policy goals and values of countries across the WHO European Region. Chapter 3 specifically highlights progress made and the common instruments and approaches to governing for equity in health through action on social determinants. What is therefore puzzling is why, despite existing efforts and good intentions, inequities persist and in some cases are increasing.

4. WHY GOVERNANCE AND DELIVERY FAIL

This chapter sets out to understand and discuss some of possible reasons for this, drawing on information gathered from key informant interviews and a review of official meeting reports and published papers for the period 2002–2012, which describe and discuss aspects of practice in governing for social determinants of health and health equity. A major finding is a lack of a "whole systems thinking" approach in governing for equity in health. To this end, a systems checklist for governing for health equity with a whole-of-government approach is put forward. This is intended for further discussion and as a framework to support strengthening country governance for health equity in practice, through action on social determinants.

Reasons for the aforementioned failure have been clustered into four main categories. These are set out in Table 4.1 and explored in more detail in the remainder of this section.

4.1. Conceptual failure

Across the WHO European Region different countries take different views of the main drivers of health inequity. These reflect political ideology and the wider socio-political circumstances and history involved, as Fig. 4.1 illustrates.

Table 4.1. Reasons for failure in governing for health equity through action on social determinants

Type of failure	Explanation
Conceptual	Failure to conceptualize the full "causal pathway" leading to the desired equity goals/outcomes.
Delivery chain	Failure to understand or construct an effective "delivery chain" capable of acting on multiple determinants to reduce inequities/increase equity in health over time.
Control strategy	Failure to develop an effective "control strategy" capable of holding stakeholders and policies to account for equity results.
Public health system	Failure to develop competences needed to govern for health as a societal objective, not only as a health sector objective.

Many countries referenced common conceptual frameworks as having influenced their thinking on health inequities, determinants and the subsequent interventions that feature in their policies and practice. These included the work of Dahlgren & Whitehead *(27)*, often referred to as the rainbow model, Graham *(28)* and WHO Global Commission on Social Determinants of Health *(29)*, as shown in Fig. 4.2.

A common feature across all the cited conceptual models is the interaction between a range of determinants which shape the causal pathways to equity/inequity within the population. Despite reference to these conceptual frameworks, in practice the connections between social position, social structures, material factors and individual behaviours are not generally clearly conceptualized or articulated in the frameworks underpinning action to reduce inequities across many European countries. Recent reviews by the WHO European Office for Investment for Health and Development of the WHO Regional Office for Europe in 2010 and 2011[8] found that the explanations for how health inequities occur and persist in society vary, but overall there is a tendency across many countries participating in the

---

[8] For details see the Bibliography.

reviews to focus on intermediate or proximal determinants. These include access to health services, lifestyle or behaviour, living conditions (such as housing and water sanitation), and social cohesion.

Fig. 4.1. WHO European Region countries' different views of the main drivers of health inequities

Health Inequalities Strategy

Different countries take different views of the main drivers of health inequalities reflecting wider socio-political drivers and history

What are the main determinants of the observed inequalities in health in your country?

Sweden
- Employment
- Education
- Flaws in distribution of resources according to need
- Weakening of social connectivity/cohesion

Spain
- Employment and work conditions
- Poverty
- Gaps in welfare state for women
- Growing problems related to obesity, smoking, alcohol
- Environment (injuries, pollution)

United Kingdom
- Poverty of resources
- Poverty of expectation (professionals, not just poor)
- Wide socioeconomic inequalities
- Powerlessness

Poland
- Uncontrolled market
- Inequalities in access to resources for health
- Failures in accountability (value base/bribery)

Source: Whitehead et al. *(30).*

A recent study *(31)* reviewing the paradox of persistent health inequities hypothesized that their persistence in modern European welfare states can partly be seen as a failure of these welfare states to implement more radical redistribution measures, and partly as a form of "bad luck" related to concurrent developments that have changed the composition of

Why governance and delivery fail

socioeconomic groups and made health inequities more sensitive to psychosocial factors. The study suggests that inequities in parts of Europe are persisting owing to a failure to conceptualize and act on the optimal mix of determinants and with the magnitude and intensity necessary to impact on their distribution.

Fig. 4.2. Commission on Social Determinants of Health conceptual framework

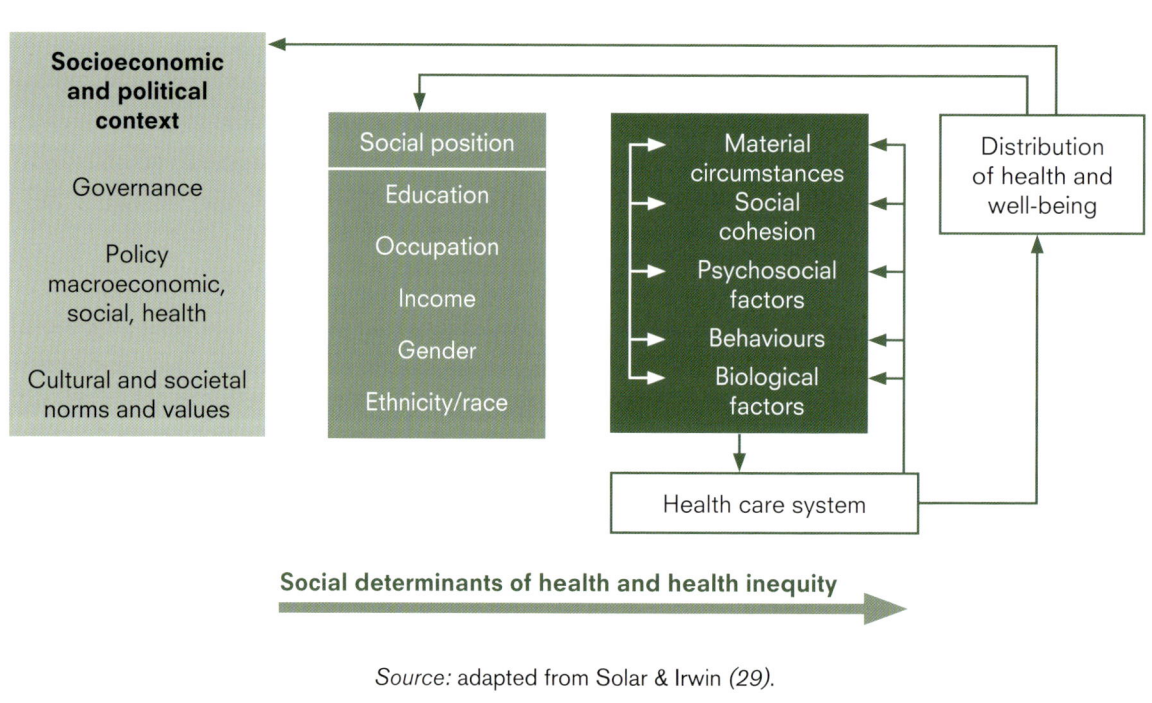

Source: adapted from Solar & Irwin (29).

This reason for failure was reflected in the findings of the United Kingdom's National Audit Office (NAO), in reviewing why England had failed to achieve its national health inequity targets for 2010. NAO reported that an important issue was the failure to sufficiently acknowledge, conceptualize and effectively address the full causal chain of poor health outcomes *(32)*. A review of the literature and key informant interviews suggest that this is a likely reason for results being poorer than expected for health inequity strategies, policies and interventions in many countries across Europe.

Explanations of how health inequities arise and persist over time are shaped not only by scientific evidence and models but by political ideology and the interests of different stakeholders with access to decision-making arenas. These drivers are important and currently include a resurgence of the "trickle down" effect: that is, a belief that policy benefits will gradually reach all groups in society and thus differences (inequities) are a natural result of the time it takes for policies to impact across the population. Individual responsibilities and behaviour change discourse are ever present in policy debates and in goals to reduce inequities, as recently evidenced by the attention to nudge strategies. Nudge strategies are those which aim to change physical and social environments to prompt or encourage desired behaviours, and nudge thinking derives from theories of behavioural changes in individuals, communities or whole populations. There is evidence that nudge strategies can impact on population behaviour where actions are relatively simple, such as washing hands and reducing speed whilst driving. However, in general they do not address the underlying causes of unequal exposure to risk: that is, social determinants, such as housing conditions, road infrastructure and design of safe urban and rural residential areas. A further influence on explaining inequity in health comes from a more practical perspective, linked to what it is deemed possible to change. In some countries, while many factors and their interactions in producing equity/inequity are acknowledged, decisions are sometimes made on the basis of what it is possible to achieve. This is more evident in countries where there is high level of silo working: that is, where instruments for cross-sectoral working are limited and/or where sector-specific performance is valued above that of delivering shared results. This issue is discussed in more detail in section 4.2, but is important to mention here, as it lends insight into reasons for conceptual failure.

Acting on a range of determinants which span health systems, behaviour, material conditions and structural factors in the distribution of power and resources in society, is not an easy task. National and European reviews suggest that investment in each of these domains will

Why governance and delivery fail

have different "payback" time frames – with improvements in early detection and treatment of existing undiagnosed illness in primary care showing the fastest results in improving health outcomes and reducing health inequities. However, without interventions to address the wider social determinants (and their lifestyle/behavioural consequences) there will be diminishing returns on such investment, as demand continues to increase (or is sustained) unchecked.

4.2. Delivery chain failure

Diverse and independent social systems (transport, housing, welfare, and so on) usually operate in accountability silos (accountability systems that are not cross-governmental). Yet the sum of their separate impacts on population health makes up the delivery chain for effective action on health inequities and social determinants of health. Failure to define and map how this dispersed delivery chain works is a key cause of ineffective management of interventions to reduce inequities through action on social determinants.

To reduce inequities in health, delivery systems need to be able to incentivize coherent action across stakeholders and decisions, hold decision-makers to account for impact on determinants and have capacities, instruments and processes in place (institutionalized) which will enable corrective action to be taken and policy to be sustained and adapted over time. These essential functions of a delivery system capable of improving equity in health reflect the principles of good governance set out by the UNDP and reflected in Box 4.1.

Earlier sections have highlighted how some of these principles are being implemented in countries across Europe. However, a review of European and international progress suggests the following common factors which reduce the performance of systems to deliver improvement in health equity through action on social determinants.

4.2.1. Reliance on small-scale project and pilots

There are many good examples of initiatives to improve health outcomes; many also have the intention to reduce health gaps between social groups, for example in access to health services, in employment opportunities and skills, and in health behaviours and lifestyles. However, the majority of interventions – while well meaning – are often of a pilot nature or limited to small-scale, time-limited projects. In many of these there is limited success in leveraging action across the range of determinants needed to reduce disparities. Those that do act on a range of determinants but which remain pilot or time limited, then suffer in terms of performance, as they are not able to achieve the scale and duration of action that is required to sustain impact and produce real improvement in the medium term.

> **Box 4.1. The principles of good governance**
>
> 6. **Legitimacy and voice:** that all stakeholders be included in a legitimate process of development.
> 7. **Direction:** that a clear vision is set.
> 8. **Performance:** that a measurable process and outcomes are set.
> 9. **Accountability:** that all relevant sectors are accountable for shared goals.
> 10. **Fairness:** that the governance systems proposed involve equitable processes backed by legislation.
>
> *Source:* Graham, Amos & Plumptre *(33)*, cited in WHO *(34)*, p. 16.

4.2.2. Lack of appropriate incentives and mechanisms for acting across sectors and determinants

Failure to act across the causal chain of determinants with sufficient effort to produce changes of the magnitude needed to reduce gaps has also been observed where there are national targets and inequity strategies and plans in place. Reasons for failure in these cases commonly arise from lack of appropriate incentives and supporting mechanisms which leverage action across a range of sectors and determinants, for example, shared targets and reporting linked to core budgets and processes for joint review. Often this is a design failure, when strategies and policies are being developed. Much effort is channelled into strategy development, but infrequently into assessing the capacity to deliver, specifically the human resource needs and/or the institutional mechanisms and incentives that would be critical to success. For this reason, many well-meaning and well-written policies and strategies are only partly implemented. Specific reasons for this cited by countries in meeting documents reviewed for this report suggest that there is often a good level of implementation across sectors and determinants where policy interests are more easily aligned, such as in health and social welfare, health and education. Relationships across many sectors, but specifically between health and the finance, labour, trade and development sectors are often cited by countries as being weaker. This suggests action on determinants is taking place where relationships are already good or where the benefits of policy coordination are clear. However, if action only takes place where good relationships with other sectors/ stakeholders already exist, where there is existing capacity within the systems or where these capacities can be controlled (such as within the sphere of influence of a single sector), this can limit the impact on the full range of determinants across the policy jurisdictions of many sectors and stakeholders outside of government.

This situation can be compounded by failure in the early stages of policy development to build a shared understanding and commitment to address inequities through action on social determinants. This primarily stems from underutilization of mechanisms for (i) joint diagnosis of existing problems; (ii) cross-sectoral and peer review of existing policies; and (iii) assessment of competing and complementary interests. Without these mechanisms and processes built into the policy development phase, it is more likely that the final policy will lack the commitment and leverage over necessary resources to ensure effective implementation or to span the range of determinants necessary to reduce inequities.

If this situation does arise, it often means that during active implementation there is an increase in demand-based interaction between health and other sectors – such as "you should" or "you must do this" (for health) – a fact that is often reflected in the way implementation plans to tackle health inequity are worded. This – together with infrequent and irregular "flows" of communication between sectors due to role and capacity deficits – further (i) hampers opportunities to act on common determinants that produce benefits for many sectors; and (ii) undermines the need to position equity as a goal for the whole of government, with health equity as one measure of progress.

4.2.3. Lack of investment in ongoing assessment of trends in inequities and social determinants

A further consequence is the missed opportunity to foster new understanding of complex problems (such as inequities) and to generate effective solutions. This can contribute to **path dependency**, whereby ways of doing things – including understanding and tackling problems – are inherited across policy cycles and reforms, often referred to as **inherited wisdom**. Emerging evidence suggests that determinants interact in different ways over time to produce the pathways which sustain or alter the nature and magnitude of inequities in health. The current lack of investment in ongoing assessment of trends in inequities and in social determinants may play a significant role in explaining why interventions are not delivering intended results.

4.2.4. Gaps in quality and type of data/intelligence

While data on demographic trends and morbidity and mortality are generally reliable, a significant weakness for the purpose of addressing social determinants is the lack of health information broken down by socioeconomic status, such as income, employment status and education. This limits monitoring of interventions and assessments of non-health sector policies on health. It also restricts the capacity of public health ministers and professionals to implement, evaluate and advocate effective policies and interventions which target the underlying social and economic causes of health in general and health inequities more specifically.

Research evidence, data and information are only some of the influences on policy decisions about equity and health. Measurement is necessary to track the consequences of policy decisions in terms of narrowing (or widening) inequities in health. In order for health intelligence for equity to be sustainable, infrastructural support is required both in terms of information technology and capacity building. The 2010 Spanish Presidency of the EU, *Moving forward equity in health – monitoring and analysis of social determinants*, highlighted how many countries across the EU community face major challenges in this regard *(35)*. This is also true for other subregions of Europe. A summer school on monitoring and analysis of health inequities, co-organized by Košice Institute for Society and Health, Pavol Jozef Šafárik University and WHO European Office for Investment for Health and Development also found similar challenges in countries of central and eastern Europe and the Balkans *(36)*. The simple consequence is that countries cannot improve what they do not measure.

The discussion on reasons why delivery systems fail highlights two major learning points. First, there is a need to consider delivery systems and mechanisms in parallel to the policy development process, as well as before policies and interventions are launched. Second, a combination of mechanisms and institutional structures is necessary. These need to be integral to core institutional arrangements, which suggests a need to work within existing systems but, importantly, to adapt these to improve performance to deliver equity results across sectors and determinants.

More broadly, this requires an understanding of the **delivery chain**, which is made up of a complex network of strategy, policy, programmes and projects. These are generally led or managed by central and local governments, with the overall aim of delivering on agreed outcomes. While orchestrated by governments, delivery chains for reducing inequities through action on social determinants also need to take account of and involve the actions of local people, civic society, the public and the private sector. This reflects a more diverse and extended delivery chain, which has its roots in social, political and economic structures across society. The delivery chain can therefore be described as being embedded within the structures (the anatomy) and systems (the physiology) of society. The former are most effective when legislatively defined, and politically led. The latter are socially constructed and informed through communications and relationships *(37)*. The challenge in governing for health equity through action on social determinants is thus to put in place instruments and processes which are capable of connecting and aligning legislative, institutional, organizational, professional, economic, cultural and social capacity across society. The aim is to produce a public good: that is, equity in health.

GOVERNANCE FOR HEALTH EQUITY

Characteristics of effective delivery systems include those defined in Box 4.2.

> **Box 4.2. Effective delivery mechanisms**
>
> An effective delivery system has the following features:
>
> - defined levers and incentives that are fit for purpose;
> - specific arrangements for managing risks to delivery;
> - performance management systems to keep delivery on track;
> - strong leadership that is politically accountable to the community it serves through clear governance structures at all levels of the delivery chain;
> - mechanisms for regular feedback and review to support continuous learning;
> - clear systems built into the delivery chain, in order to:
>   - achieve efficiency;
>   - reduce transaction costs;
>   - share services and utilize common assets;
>   - engage with commercial/private sector (especially suppliers);
>   - enable a designed regulatory regime capable of driving good performance;
>   - reduce tiers of administration;
>   - assess how best to integrate multiple sources of service delivery to citizens;
>   - co-produce outcomes with the public;
> - a high level of visibility, as well as producing reports in the public domain that are capable of stimulating participatory citizen action for improvement.
>
> *Source:* adapted from NAO & Audit Commission (37).

4.3. Governmental control strategy failure

Many systems established by government have failed to deliver sustained and systematic improvements in health equity. Conceptual failure and delivery chain failure have been discussed in the previous sections, but a third facet exists: failure to develop an effective "control strategy" capable of holding all stakeholders to account for delivery of actions necessary to reduce inequities.

An effective control strategy would define actions required by all sectors in producing equity results. It would also specify the appropriate instruments: that is, the sanctions and rewards which are important to mitigate failure and sustain action on social determinants over time. In this way, an effective control strategy is one designed to control both actions (inputs) and results (outputs). As stated throughout this report, reducing inequities in health requires coherence of action across many stakeholders, many of whom are not involved formally in government. As such, the instruments which make for an effective control strategy need to be multiple and embedded within different arenas of society. However, government at the national and local levels has a primary role to ensure these instruments are in place and operating effectively.

To this end, this report argues the strong need for a formal agency with the mandated role and capacity to ensure that accountability for equity (actions and results) is in place and operating effectively. Such an agency would need to have capacity for generating the research and evidence necessary to inform equity reporting. In addition, it would need civic or legislative powers that allowed it to comment on, influence or control the actions of many sectors (health, transport, housing, and so on). Many countries across the WHO European Region do not have an agency with this kind of capacity. Many have elements of a control strategy but the mix and coherence of instruments seems inadequate for the complexity or scale of the challenge. For example, in many countries public health laws and constitutional frameworks exist, which serve to enforce equality of opportunity to participate in society (employment, education) and/or which guarantee conditions that secure population health (clean water, safe housing). However, the necessary complements to ensure laws are acted upon – including intelligence, regulatory instruments, transparent reporting, policy adjustment tools and participatory models of planning – are frequently lacking, uncoordinated or not systematically used with regard to equity impacts. This control strategy failure means that the health equity outcome of much of government decision- and policy-making is effectively "unmanaged". This gives further impetus for strengthening existing agency capacity or establishing new agencies, with the mandated role of ensuring that accountability for equity (actions and results) is in place and operating effectively.

This function could be carried out either at national level or, in countries with a high level of decentralization, the function could be established at the most appropriate level of political accountability.

4.4. Public health system failure

Governing for equity in health through action on social determinants demands new roles for ministries of health and the public health community. The whole-of-government and whole-of-society approaches necessary to improve and sustain equity require that governments and public health professionals take on diverse roles. This includes: overall leader with responsibility for imposing mandatory regulations that define norms and rules for consumers and all stakeholders; provider of public goods and services; steward of public resources; and partner in collaborative work with other policy sectors, businesses, and civil society organizations *(38)*. Many of these functions have been recently debated across Europe, with the WHO Regional Office for Europe *(39)* and the EU *(40)* both producing new guidance documents to modernize public health in Europe.

While not the main focus of this report, drawing on new guidance in Europe and including a review of public health practice and functions suggest that certain roles are essential to address inequities through action on social determinants. These roles are outlined in the paragraphs that follow.

Building and sustaining a narrative for health equity – which connects to broader sectoral, governmental and societal goals – is essential. Such a narrative must be capable of embedding health equity into main government strategies and financial mechanisms, which requires capacities to: (i) stimulate debates in parliament, in cabinet committees and in the media; (ii) ensure clear multi-stakeholder mechanisms for accountability, such as arms-length independent bodies and formal consultative groups; and (iii) make documents and decision processes/outcomes available.

A small dedicated resource unit is necessary to keep the issue "live" and move across communities and sectors freely, with the aim of promoting regular dialogue and platforms for debate on determinants, as well as identifying where policy synergies or countervailing agendas exist. In this, the unit would act as part of the governance system, which also has a role in assessing and stimulating debate on trends in determinants and health equity and in giving voice and action to these in decision-making arenas (such as policy and political briefings; in the media; and through scientific journals and fora).

The major intelligence role should include evidence and analyses to support ministries of health in generating and adapting the strategic narrative for equity and in the generation and testing of policy options. One approach to focus on is applying a health (equity) "lens" across government policies, using tools such as impact assessment, distribution modelling and scenario development, to test the efficacy of policies under certain conditions. Increasingly, this intelligence role is part of a network of institutions contributing different forms of information and analysis to support decision-making and review.

Developing, coordinating and supporting policy learning and capacity building include action on guidance, systematic reviews with other partners and producing reports on progress. It also involves developing learning support materials, and organizing on-the-job training and review. Support could be given to knowledge development and exchange during implementation, through a range of process and policy evaluation methodologies.

In developing the new public health strategy for Europe, the WHO Regional Office for Europe in partnership with Member States identified a mismatch between current public health practice and that which is necessary to be effective in protecting and promoting health and health equity, where many influences stem from social determinants and socio-economic factors that lay outside the direct control of ministries of health. This includes weak and/or uneven progress in developing public health systems and capacities that are capable of delivering these critical actions.

Applying and extending this analysis to governance and delivery of social determinants of health and health inequity, it is possible to summarize the new domains of civic agency (public leadership and action) for effective public health, as shown in Table 4.2.

Table 4.2. New domains of civic agency for public health

	Civic agency function	Domain
1.	Governance regulator	Health governance
2.	Enabler of whole-of-government/whole-of-society action	Health delivery
3.	Foresight management	Health foresight
4.	Resilience management	Health resilience/Health protection
5.	Enabler of social enterprises/corporate social responsibility/new prevention and early intervention enterprises	Health innovation
6.	Community asset developer	Health assets
7.	Advocate/enabler of public and political demand for change	Health advocate
8.	Partner in multi-sectoral collaboration	Health coalitions
9.	Steward of public resources for investment	Health services
10.	Provider of public goods and services	Health improvement
11.	Researcher	Health research
12.	Knowledge transfer/brokerage/training	Health knowledge broker

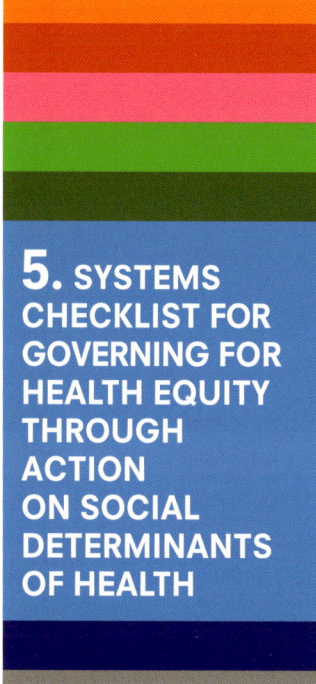

5. SYSTEMS CHECKLIST FOR GOVERNING FOR HEALTH EQUITY THROUGH ACTION ON SOCIAL DETERMINANTS OF HEALTH

This chapter sets out a systems checklist for governing for health equity as a whole-of-government and whole-of-society approach. It builds on the findings and issues set out in the previous chapters, and is intended (i) for further discussion and (ii) as a draft framework to support strengthening how governing for health equity is carried out in practice through action on social determinants. It also draws on other evidence-based frameworks and governance tools, including the work of the Public Health Agency of Canada on necessary steps for the implementation of intersectoral action on health (see Table 5.1), the work of Valentine et al. *(41)* on translating the social determinants of health agenda in action at the country level and the work of Brown et al. in developing the forthcoming resource guide on governance for social determinants of health and health inequities.

Table 5.1. Necessary steps for successful implementation of intersectoral action

	Steps
1.	Create a policy framework and an approach to health that are conductive to intersectoral action.
2.	Emphasize shared values, interests, and objectives among partners and potential partners.
3.	Ensure political support; build on positive factors in the policy environment.
4.	Engage key partners at the very beginning; be inclusive.
5.	Ensure appropriate horizontal linking across sectors as well as vertical linking of levels within sectors.
6.	Invest in the alliance-building process by working towards consensus at the planning stage.
7.	Focus on concrete objectives and visible results.
8.	Ensure that leadership, accountability, and rewards are shared among partners.
9.	Build stable teams of people who work well together, with appropriate support system.
10.	Develop pratical models, tools, and mechanisms to support the implementation of intersectoral action.
11	Ensure public partecipation; educate the public and raise awareness about health determinants and intersectoral action.

Source: Public Health Agency of Canada *(42)*, cited in WHO *(34)*, p. 15.

On the basis of this evidence and the previous analysis reviewed in this report, it is possible to define the characteristics or functions of governance systems which are effective in addressing social determinants and reducing inequities in health. Table 5.2 summarizes these.

Table 5.2. Functions and characteristics important in governing for equity in health through action on social determinants

Domain	Systems characteristic	Exemplified by
1. Political commitment	• Clear political commitment	1.1 Ministerial accountability for governance and delivery of SD/HI[a] 1.2 Specific political roles for SD/HI at national, regional and local levels 1.3 Cross-government committee for SD and Equity 1.4 Explicit budget for SD/HI management 1.5 Institutional and legislative framework for equity in health and development
2. Intelligence	Evidence and information to: a) inform policy and investment decisions b) monitor progress c) hold stakeholders to account. Specifically, in terms of: • research and intelligence on SD/HI trends and policies; • the effectiveness of governance and delivery systems; • metrics, i.e. targets/indicators for improvement in health equity and distribution of SD at European, national and local levels	2.1 SD/HI as a core work and funding stream in research budgets 2.2 SD/HI evidence systematically reviewed and publicly reported 2.3 Dedicated health intelligence and analysis services producing open access data 2.4 Input, output and outcomes data published on SD/HI at local, national and European levels 2.5 Agreed minimum data sets/reporting requirements, on SD, equity and health inequities for national and local levels

[a] SD = social determinants. HI = health inequity.

Table 5.2. contd

Domain	Systems characteristic	Exemplified by
3. Accountability structures and systems	• Legislative structures and systems enabling intersectoral action on SD and health inequities at European, national and local levels • Statutory "governance boards" capable of holding all stakeholders to account • Legislative structures and systems enabling formation and action of NGOs and civil society groups as partners in action to reduce inequities and monitoring progress	3.1 A legal framework involving a duty placed on all health and non-health stakeholders, to collaborate and report on SD/HI actions and outcomes 3.2 Community health status/outcome (SD/HI) boards, established with explicit powers to review data/progress of policies, review options/solutions for improving health equity and to hold all stakeholders to account 3.3 Statutory roles with a formal duty to reduce inequities through action on SD, i.e. empowered to publicly mandate action at European, national and local levels (public health minister, chair of parliamentary development committee, prime minister, ombudsman)
4. Policy coherence across government sectors and levels	• A formal and explicit framework setting out stakeholders and policy action for improving equity in health and development (SD) • Framework will be linked to ministerial portfolios and budgets, nationally and locally • Government policy audited through health impact assessment and equity impact assessment • Instruments which institutionalize collaboration across sectors and levels of government	4.1 Coherence of sectoral actions (national and local) on agreed SD and equity targets 4.2 Outcomes, explicitly defined for all government and sectoral spending, nationally and locally 4.3 Specific agreements with the private sector (industry/commerce) on their contribution to delivering equity targets 4.4 Outcomes assessed and published by all ministries/directorates at all levels of governance 4.5 Impact assessments, which should be public domain documents, challengeable through accountability mechanisms 4.6. Systems for joint accounting for results in place, including pooled budgets, shared targets, joint review and reporting on progress, integrated intelligence systems

Table 5.2. contd

Domain	Systems characteristic	Exemplified by
5. Involving local people	• Commitment to participation of local people and subnational authorities in policy design and review • Instruments and systems which secure community involvement in solutions • Intelligence and data on health, equity and SD made accessible within the public domain – locally, nationally and across Europe	5.1 Mechanisms, organizational design and capacity building to enable diversity of voices and perspectives from the community and local level in local decision-making and solutions 5.2 Representatives at all levels of SD/HI governance, who should be equal members alongside professional members of decision-making committees 5.3 Tools, instruments and support at the local level to define local problems and solutions, informed by local data 5.4 Public reporting of actions and progress to allow access to and debate on results and new challenges, by and with community/third parties
6. Institutional and human resource capacity	• Capacity development, including: - development of competent and trained SD/HI staff - institutional processes - formal accountability, annual publishing of progress results	6.1 Programmes supporting political, civic and professional leadership of SD/HI within different institutional and social systems of society, locally, nationally and in Europe 6.2 Curriculum modules on equity, health and SD in professional and vocational training, within and outside the health sector 6.3 Formal protocols defining institutional arrangements and expectations related to SD/HI in all sectors
7. Modernized public health	• Review and modernization of public health training and practice	7.1 Revised descriptors and competences for national public health practice 7.2 Revised descriptors for domains of public health intervention (with an increased focus on the use of new social media technology, management of social change and citizen mobilization) 7.3 New/updated training for public health professionals

Systems checklist for governing for health equity through action on social determinants of health

Table 5.2. contd

Domain	Systems characteristic	Exemplified by
8. Learning and innovation systems	• Commitment to continuous improvement in understanding of SD, equity and the efficacy of policies and interventions to reduce inequities • Commitment to ongoing performance review/improvements in governing for equity in health, through action on SD	8.1 Stronger learning transfer systems within and between countries, in order to accelerate uptake of promising policies and governance instruments 8.2 Enriched national and European capacity to tackle inequities in health through establishing multi-country innovation programmes, live demonstration sites/exchanges, along with documented and disseminated learning 8.3 Established European registry of policies and governance systems addressing inequities through action on SD

The checklist does not seek to prescribe an ideal or "best" governance structure which countries should adopt. Instead, it draws out a set of general functions which need to be embedded in the governance arrangements of a country in order to deliver improved equity in health through action on social determinants. The functions are generic. This is deliberate and in recognition that further debate and work in this area are needed to enable appropriate adaptation of recommendations to different policy-making levels across diverse cultures, traditions and development conditions of the Member States in the WHO European Region.

5.1. Characteristics of delivery systems important to reducing inequities through action on social determinants of health

While identifying the characteristics of effective governance for health is crucial, such systems can only bear fruit if there is a delivery system to enable action to be taken across the levels, systems and sectors that are subject to governance.

Some of the functions of an effective social determinants of health/health inequity delivery system overlap with those of an effective governance system. Table 5.3 shows the key delivery systems characteristics.

Table 5.3. Key delivery systems characteristics

Delivery function	Delivery systems characteristics
1. Defined delivery chain	The delivery chain for social determinants of health/health inequities is explicit, understood, described, owned, supported or managed by the relevant stakeholders.
2. Ownership and active management	The delivery system has an explicit control loop managed by a defined owner (governance system/Minister/professional) with positional authority, whose aim is to identify and correct both risks to delivery and outcome failures.
3. Levers and incentives	The system has defined levers and incentives available to both the manager and the system stakeholders.
4. Performance management	The system has a performance management system with appropriate metrics and systems for research, data collection, monitoring and evaluation related to input/output processes and outcomes.
5. Strong leadership	The delivery system has strong leadership that is politically accountable to the community it serves through clear governance structures at all levels of the delivery chain.
6. Sustainable financing and training	The system is adequately and sustainably financed within a statutory institutional framework and has staff that are appropriately trained.
7. Political support and statutory responsibilities	The delivery system has both political support and functional independence. It has the statutory responsibilities and authority necessary to require delivery action from all relevant stakeholders in the delivery chain.
8. High public visibility and engagement	The system has high public and political visibility with a strong media (and digital) presence. It is capable of mobilizing wider society to use the data it controls in order to support change from delivery chain stakeholders (i.e. to generate popular demand for change through mechanisms of monitory democracy (see section 2.4)).
9. Annual reporting	The system reports annually to the public it serves, identifying obstacles to progress and proposed corrective actions attributable to named individuals and institutions.
10. Development support and public scrutiny	The system works both through prospective developmental interventions (working with stakeholders to improve their functional performance in the delivery chain) and through methods involving corrective scrutiny (publicly identifying culpable failure and the consequences thereof).
11. Metrics, research and evaluation	The delivery system commissions relevant research and evaluation, and has clear metrics and mechanisms for regular process input, output and outcome reviews and continuous reflective learning (an internal improvement control loop). This is captured and reported upon on an annual basis.

Systems checklist for governing for health equity through action on social determinants of health

6. RECOMMENDATIONS

6.1. Promote and ensure shared responsibility for equity results across government

Policy in every sector of government can potentially affect health. Although health may not be the explicit focus in many policy areas, unless the equity and health effects of policies and investments are considered, opportunities are being missed for reducing inequities in health through action on social determinants. Coordinated action between sectors has the potential to contribute to significant health gains.

Governing for equity in health therefore involves a commitment not only to a value of health but also to the concept of "equity in all policies". This is a way of achieving mutual benefits that accrue to multiple sectors, as well as a public good that produces benefits for the whole of society.

This report argues that the health equity outcomes of much of government policy and decision-making are currently largely unmanaged. In part this stems from an imbalance in the mix of incentives and instruments used to align actions across policy sectors and between government and other stakeholders. Formal accountability mechanisms – which are backed up by supportive incentives – show the most promise to ensure cross-sectoral policy development, implementation and review. These mechanisms are examined in the paragraphs that follow.

6.1.1. Strengthening the mix and coherence of instruments which enable and reward joint action on social inequities (i) across sectoral portfolios and (ii) between local, regional and national governments

- Implement a formal cross-government framework (for example, a strategy), setting out explicit goals and policy actions of different sectors and levels of administration for reducing social inequities in health and development (and linked to ministerial portfolios and budgets nationally and locally).

- Use existing or develop new legislation, regulation and memoranda of understanding to set and monitor the requirements of sectors across government in delivering agreed goals relating to equity and health.

- Put in place joint accounting for results, including shared targets, joint review and reporting on progress.

- Systematize the use of structured impact assessments – to better inform and evaluate policy and investment decisions on determinants of equity and health.

- Introduce or scale up financial and reward systems linked to team results, such as pooled and shared budgets.

- Produce new or further strengthen existing guidance and support mechanisms which enable different stakeholders to implement actions on social determinants and health equity. Information, evidence, guidance and training are important features of supportive systems that can facilitate action.

6.2. Accountability instruments and capacities for equity

At both global and country levels, a wide range of social, technological, political and cultural factors are making effective governance a more complex task, as the "locus of control" for governance dissipates across societies.

At the global level, there is a trend for governments to cede national control and sovereignty to international trade agreements, multinational companies and wider legislative frameworks established on the basis of (quasi-)political and legislative unions, such as with the EU. This highlights how national policy commitment to equity in health and social determinants of health is increasingly shaped by factors and agencies beyond local and national borders.

Within national borders, decentralization of responsibilities to authorities at the subnational levels, plus new models of partnership between government, private sector and tertiary sector organizations are increasingly common features of governance systems across Europe. These changes have increased the number stakeholders and arenas in which decisions are being made, many of which have the potential to positively or negatively impact on determinants of health and health inequities.

This report argues that government has a critical role to play in determining the conditions through which health governance and delivery of improvements in the social determinants of health and health equity are achieved. It argues the need for countries (and pan-European organizations) to strengthen their capacities and combinations of instruments which are capable of holding all stakeholders to account for equity results.

- Use existing or develop new legislation, regulation and memoranda of understanding to set the requirements of stakeholders in delivering agreed goals on equity and health (and monitor implementation of these requirements).

- Strengthen the capacity and remit of existing statutory governance bodies to hold all stakeholders to account. These should have access to competent and well-trained public health scientists, be required to report on findings and have the authority to propose remedial action.

- Enhance the role of government and ministry of health policy units to collect and make available data on health, disaggregated by social and economic factors.

- Implement health intelligence systems that draw on and use a range of data sources to inform analysis, reporting and implementation of action on social determinants. These include household surveys, censuses, vital registrations (births, deaths), institution-based data (individual, service or resource records), and case studies.

- Specify agreements with the private sector (industry/commerce) on their contribution to delivering equity targets.

- Scale up and strengthen programmes supporting political, civic and professional leadership of social determinants of health and equity at local and national levels.

6.3. Equity and health equity as indicators of a fair and sustainable society

Governance of social determinants is important, not only in terms of preventing and mitigating the effects of actions which are likely to produce inequity in health, but also in terms of its role in positioning and sustaining health and health equity as important assets which contribute to the attainment of other societal goals and values (such as shared societal goods).

This is because many of the determinants of health equity/inequity are also shared priorities for other sectors and government/society. This includes goals such as social inclusion/cohesion, poverty reduction, sustainable development and community resilience. These goals provide a convergence point for common action across government and society. If due attention to their distribution is given it can produce benefits for many sectors, including for health and health equity.

For these reasons a key goal in governing for equity in health through action on social determinants is to create and sustain political support for equity as a societal good.

Ministries of health and the public health community have a key role to play to create and support a strong case for why improving equity and action on social determinants are priorities, not only for health but also for the attainment of other government/societal goals and aspirations. This can be achieved by:

- building and sustaining a strong case for health equity which connects to broader sectoral, governmental and societal goals (which requires capacities and intelligence, including evidence and analysis, in order to stimulate debates in parliament, in cabinet committees and in the media);

- using joint assessment methods in partnership with other sectors and stakeholders within and outside of government, including local communities. These should aim to build support for a common understanding of problems and of possible solutions to address social inequities and health improvement.

6.4. Involving local people and communities improves the design and impact of policies and investments aimed at improving health and reducing social inequities

There is often a lack of understanding of the social, cultural and economic lives of the resource poor population when policies are being designed. The result is interventions which are often mismatched to the realities of people's lives and can fall short of delivering intended benefits for those most in need. In some cases the consequences are to unintentionally benefit some groups more than others, thus widening gaps in health within countries.

For these reasons this report argues the need to develop new and/or strengthened instruments and mechanisms that ensure equity of voice and perspectives in decision-making processes. Specifically, emphasis should be placed on ensuring that the differential needs of marginalized and at-risk groups are recognized, and that they are involved in resource allocations as well as the design, monitoring and review of policies, services and interventions.

In doing so health equity governance could also contribute to promoting and supporting social inclusion and social justice in a given society, by:

- providing and supporting local people and communities to build capacity to participate in local decision-making and develop solutions which inform policies and investments at local and national levels;

- strengthening the capacity of NGOs and local authorities in their use of participatory planning methods which improve health and reduce social inequities;

- using tools and instruments to provide support to the local level in order to define local problems and solutions, informed by local data;

- public reporting of actions and progress to allow access to and debate on results and new challenges, by and with community/third parties;

- making intelligence and data on health, equity and social determinants accessible within the public domain – locally and nationally.

6.5. Europe-wide information exchange

Information exchange across Europe should be promoted based on innovative approaches, trends and effective interventions for improving equity in health through action on social determinants, including:

- establishing a European registry of policies and governance systems addressing inequities through action on social determinants;

- strengthening and expanding learning transfer systems within and between countries, which will accelerate the uptake of promising policies and governance approaches to address social determinants of health and health equity;

- increasing capacity to anticipate and respond to the health equity effects of emerging social, economic, political and cultural trends in society, using foresight methods including futures modelling and scenario-based policy analysis in order to react more quickly and adapt to changes which may affect attainment of policy priorities;

- brokering and supporting policy research alliances on social determinants of health between the east and west and between the north and south of the WHO European Region.

7. REFERENCES

1. *Overcoming inequality: why governance matters*. Paris, United Nations Educational Scientific and Cultural Organization 2009.

2. Kickbusch I et al. *Governance for health in the 21st century: a study conducted for the WHO Regional Office for Europe*. Copenhagen, WHO Regional Office for Europe, 2011 (http://www.euro.who.int/__data/assets/pdf_file/0010/148951/RC61_InfDoc6.pdf, accessed 15 October 2012).

3. European Health for All database (HFA-DB) [online database]. Copenhagen, WHO Regional Office for Europe, July 2013 update (http://www.euro.who.int/hfadb, accessed 18 September 2013).

4. European Health for All database (HFA-DB) [online database]. Copenhagen, WHO Regional Office for Europe, January 2013 update (http://www.euro.who.int/hfadb, accessed 3 June 2013).

5. *World health statistics 2011*. Geneva, World Health Organization, 2011 (http://www.who.int/whosis/whostat/2011/en/index.html, accessed 15 October 2012).

6. Hosseinpoor AR et al. Socioeconomic inequality in the prevalence of noncommunicable diseases in low- and middle-income countries: results from the World Health Survey. *BMC Public Health*, 2012, 12:474.

7. Braveman P, Tarimo E. Social inequalities in health within countries: not only an issue for affluent nations. *Social Science and Medicine*, 2002, 54(11):1621–1635.

8. *Poverty and social exclusion in the WHO European Region: health systems respond*. Copenhagen, WHO Regional Office for Europe, 2010 (http://www.euro.who.int/__data/assets/pdf_file/0006/115485/E94018.pdf, accessed 15 October 2012).

9. Gwatkin DR. Reducing health inequalities in developing countries. In: Detels R, et al., eds. *Oxford textbook of public health*. Vol. 3, 4th ed. New York, NY, Oxford University Press, 2002:1791–1810.

10. Lin V. Economic growth, economic decline and implications for health in all policies. *Public Health Bulletin SA*, 2010, 7(2):40–42.

11. Marmot M. *Fair society, healthy lives: the Marmot review. Strategic review of health inequalities in England post-2010*. London, University College London Institute of Health Equity, 2010 (http://www.instituteofhealthequity.org/projects/fair-society-healthy-lives-the-marmot-review, accessed 15 October 2012).

12. *Constitution of the World Health Organization.* Geneva, World Health Organization, 22 July 1946 (http://whqlibdoc.who.int/hist/official_records/constitution.pdf, accessed 20 January 2013).

13. *Universal Declaration of Human Rights.* New York, NY, General Assembly of the United Nations, 1948 (http://www.unhcr.org/refworld/docid/3ae6b3712c.html, accessed 20 January 2013).

14. *International Covenant on Economic, Social and Cultural Rights. United Nations General Assembly resolution 2200A (XXI).* Geneva, Office of the United Nations High Commissioner for Human Rights, 1966 (http://www2.ohchr.org/english/law/pdf/cescr.pdf, accessed 20 January 2013)

15. Taipale I et al., eds. *War or health: a reader.* London, Zed Books, 2002.

16. UNECE et al. *The MDGs in Europe and central Asia: achievements, challenges and the way forward.* Geneva, United Nations Economic Commission for Europe, 2010 (http://www.unece.org/commission/MDGs/2010_MDG.pdf, accessed 15 October 2012).

17. *Towards human resilience: sustaining MDG progress in an age of economic uncertainty.* New York, NY, United Nations Development Programme, 2011 (http://www.undp.org/content/dam/undp/library/Poverty%20Reduction/Towards_SustainingMDG_Web1005.pdf, accessed 15 October 2012).

18. Mackenback JP, Meerding WJ, Kunst AE. *Economic implications of socio-economic inequalities in health in the European Union.* Brussels, European Communities Directorate-General for Health and Consumer Protection, 2007:4–5.

19. Suhrcke M, Rocco L, McKee M. *Health: a vital investment for economic development in eastern Europe and central Asia.* Copenhagen, WHO Regional Office for Europe on behalf of the European Observatory on Health Systems and Policies, 2007 (http://www.euro.who.int/__data/assets/pdf_file/0003/74739/E90569.pdf, accessed 15 October 2012).

20. McDaid D, Sassi F, Merkur S, eds. *The economic case for public health action.* Maidenhead, Open University Press (in press).

21. Lister G et al. *The societal costs of potentially preventable illnesses: a rapid review.* London, National Social Marketing Centre, 2006.

22. Performance and single outcome agreements [web site]. Edinburgh, The Scottish Government, 2011 (http://www.scotland.gov.uk/Topics/Government/local-government/delperf/SOA, accessed 15 October 2012).

23. *Tackling health inequalities: a programme for action*. London, Department of Health, 2005.

24. *The Norwegian Public Health Act*. Oslo, Norwegian Ministry of Health and Care Services, 2011 (ACT-2011-06-24-29) (http://www.regjeringen.no/upload/HOD/Hoeringer%20FHA_FOS/123.pdf, accessed 9 April 2012).

25. Roberts H, Smith SJ, Bryce C. *Children at risk? Safety as a social value*. Buckingham, Open University Press, 1995.

26. Popay J et al. *Understanding and tackling social exclusion. Final report to the WHO Commission on Social Determinants of Health from the Social Exclusion Knowledge Network*. Geneva, World Health Organization, 2008 (http://www.who.int/social_determinants/knowledge_networks/final_reports/sekn_final%20report_042008.pdf, accessed 15 October 2012).

27. Dahlgren G, Whitehead M. *Policies and strategies to promote social equity in health*. Copenhagen, WHO Regional office for Europe, 1992 (http://whqlibdoc.who.int/euro/-1993/EUR_ICP_RPD414(2).pdf, accessed 15 October 2012) (EUR/ICP/RPD 414(2)).

28. Graham H. Tackling inequalities in health in England: remedying health disadvantages, narrowing health gaps or reducing health gradients? *Journal of Social Policy*, 2004, 33:115–131.

29. Solar O, Irwin A. *A conceptual framework for action on the social determinants of health. Discussion paper for the Commission on Social Determinants of Health*. Geneva, World Health Organization, 2007.

30. Whitehead M et al., eds. *Marshalling policy options and examples for tackling social determinants of inequalities in health. Report of an Expert Group Meeting hosted by the WHO Collaborating Centre for Policy Research on Social Determinants of Health*. Liverpool, University of Liverpool, 2007.

31. Mackenbach JP. The persistence of health inequalities in modern welfare states. The explanation of a paradox. *Social Science and Medicine*, 2012, 77:561–769.

32. *Tackling inequalities in life expectancy in areas with the worst health and deprivation*. London, National Audit Office, 2010 (http://www.nao.org.uk/idoc.ashx?docId=51AFDB75-B6B9-4A21-9C6A-9E9475A66333&version=-1, accessed 24 October 2012).

33. Graham J, Amos B, Plumptre T. *Principles for good governance in the 21st century. Policy brief no. 15*. Ottawa, ON, Institute on Governance, 2003 (http://iog.ca/sites/iog/files/policybrief15_0.pdf, accessed 10 November 2012).

34. *Closing the gap: policy into practice on the social determinants of health. Discussion paper.* Geneva, World Health Organization, 2011 (http://www.who.int/sdhconference/Discussion-Paper-EN.pdf, accessed 15 October 2012).

35. *Moving forward equity in health: monitoring social determinants of health and the reduction of health inequalities.* Madrid, Ministry of Health and Social Policy of Spain, 2010 (http://www.msps.es/profesionales/saludPublica/prevPromocion/promocion/desigualdadSalud/PresidenciaUE_2010/conferenciaExpertos/docs/haciaLaEquidadEnSalud_en.pdf, accessed 10 November 2012).

36. Analysis of social determinants of health and health inequities – a multi-country event on approaches and policy [web site]. Košice, Pavol Jozef Šafárik University, 2009 (http://www.lf.upjs.sk/omek/index.html, accessed 10 November 2012).

37. NAO, Audit Commission. *Delivering efficiently: strengthening the links in public service delivery chains. Report by the Comptroller and Auditor General, prepared jointly by the National Audit Office and the Audit Commission (HC 940 Session 2005–2006).* London, The Stationery Office, 2006.

38. Dubé L et al. *Building convergence: toward an integrated health and agri-food strategy for Canada.* Ottawa, ON, The Canadian Agri-Food Policy Institute (CAPI), 2009 (http://www.capi-icpa.ca/pdfs/BuildingConvergence_Summary.pdf, accessed 9 April 2012).

39. *European Action Plan for Strengthening Public Health Capacities and Services.* Copenhagen, WHO Regional Office for Europe, 2012 (http://www.euro.who.int/_data/assets/pdf_file/0005/171770/RC62wd12rev1-Eng.pdf/, accessed 28 October 2013) (EUR/RC62/12).

40. *Together for health: a strategic approach for the EU 2008–2013. White paper.* Brussels, Commission of the European Communities, 2007 (IP/07/1571) (http://europa.eu/rapid/press-release_IP-07-1571_en.htm?locale=en, accessed 15 October 2012).

41. Valentine N et al. *Health equity at the country level: lessons from the CSDH on translating a complex agenda into action.* Geneva, World Health Organization, 2008 (http://190.210.115.167/curso/cursoesp/Textos%20Completos/health%20equity%20at%20the%20country%20level.pdf, accessed 15 October 2012).

42. *Crossing sectors – experiences in intersectoral action, public policy and health.* Ottawa, ON, Public Health Agency of Canada, 2007.

8. BIBLIOGRAPHY

8th Baltic policy dialogue. Implementing integrated public health strategies to improve health and reduce health inequities. Vilnius, 2–3 November 2011 (Session 5: Addressing the social determinants of health – the state of policy response in the Baltic States). Vilnius, WHO Regional Office for Europe and European Observatory on Health Systems and Policies, 2011.

Dahlgren G, Whitehead M. Tackling inequalities in health: what can we learn from what has been tried? In: Dahlgren G, Whitehead M. *European strategies for tackling social inequities in health: levelling up part 2*. Copenhagen, WHO Regional office for Europe, 2007 (http://www.euro.who.int/__data/assets/pdf_file/0018/103824/E89384.pdf, accessed 9 April, 2012).

First WHO European conference on the new European policy for health – Health 2020. Working together across sectors for health and well-being. 28–29 November 2011. Jerusalem, WHO Regional Office for Europe, 2011 (http://www.euro.who.int/en/what-we-do/event/first-who-european-conference-on-the-new-european-policy-for-health-health-2020, accessed 15 October 2012).

Health, sustainable development and poverty reduction: WHO international consultation. Venice, 25–27 November 2004. Venice, WHO Regional Office for Europe, 2004.

Health, sustainable development and poverty reduction: review of trends and strategies in south-eastern Europe: knowledge forum. Paris, 11–13 July 2005. Paris, Council of Europe, Development Bank, Council of Europe, South-eastern Europe Health Network and WHO Regional Office for Europe, 2005.

Opportunities for scaling up and strengthening health in all policies in south-eastern Europe. Copenhagen, WHO Regional Office for Europe (in press).

Pan-European macro-drivers: work, worklessness, social protection and health inequalities. Main issues, themes and futures scanning. London, Health Action Partnership International, 2012 (http://www.equitychannel.net/uploads/EU%20Progress%20Working%20for%20Equity%20in%20Health%20-%20Macro-drivers%20paper.pdf, accessed 15 October 2012).

Poverty and health technical consultation. Follow-up to Resolution EUR/RC52/R7. Venice, 29 November to 1 December 2007. Venice, WHO Regional Office for Europe, 2007.

Poverty and social exclusion in the WHO European Region: health systems respond. Copenhagen, WHO Regional Office for Europe, 2010 (http://www.euro.who.int/__data/assets/pdf_file/0006/115485/E94018.pdf, accessed 15 October 2012).

Slovene national consultation on the interim findings and emerging themes from the WHO European review on social determinants and the health divide. Ljubljana, 6 December 2011. Ljubljana, Slovenian Ministry of Health, WHO Regional Office for Europe and University College London.

Social determinants and health: the role of national action plans in reducing health inequities. Report of a multi-country seminar: Helsinki, 17–18 November 2009. Copenhagen, WHO Regional Office for Europe, 2010 (http://www.euro.who.int/__data/assets/pdf_file/0005/125339/e94410.pdf, accessed 15 October 2012).

WHO consultation meeting to support countries in leading action to tackle the social determinants of health and health inequities. Edinburgh, 3–5 December 2006. Edinburgh, WHO Regional Office for Europe, 2006.

European forum on tackling the social determinants of health and reducing health inequities. Emerging know-how, policy options and country experiences in shaping an agenda for systematic action. London, 1–2 March 2007. London, WHO Regional Office for Europe, 2007.

Governance for social determinants of health and health equity seeks to strengthen the coherence of actions across sectors and stakeholders in a manner that increases resource flows to redress current patterns and magnitude of health inequities, and to improve the distribution of determinants in opportunity to be healthy and in risk and consequences of disease and premature mortality, across the population.